Friends & Recipes

JACKIE ALLISS

Friends & Recipes

Lennard Publishing
1988

Lᴇɴɴᴀʀᴅ Pᴜʙʟɪsʜɪɴɢ
a division of Lennard Books Ltd
92, Hastings Street,
Luton,
Beds LU1 5BH

First published 1988
Copyright © Jackie Alliss 1988

Alliss, Jackie
    Friends and recipes.
    1. Food – Recipes
    I. Title
    641.5

    ISBN 1-85291-030-5

Editor Michael Leitch
Jacket design by Pocknell & Co
Text design and setting by Nuprint Ltd
Printed and bound in Great Britain by
Butler & Tanner, Frome, Somerset

Contents

The Recipes

Recipes for the dishes picked out in bold type can be found in the second half of the book among many other personal and family favourites.

CHAPTER ONE

CONFESSIONS OF A RECIPE COLLECTOR

I WAS STANDING UNDER a colourful golf umbrella in the pouring rain at the Dalmahoy Golf Club a few miles east of Edinburgh. It was the late July of 1965, the Gallaher Senior Service Golf Tournament was in full swing and the course was 'awash'. Play had been cancelled and as I surveyed the dank and dripping scene, little did I know that the handsome golfer I was later to be introduced to at the clubhouse bar would, in years ahead, become my husband.

Nineteen-sixty-five was a special year in so many ways for me. I was young, had recently completed a short spell of auxiliary nursing at Stratford-upon-Avon Hospital, had broken off an engagement that I think we both had doubts about, and now, with enormous luck, I had managed to land a marvellous job on the Sales Promotion team of the Gallaher Tobacco Company.

I was single, brimful of energy, and life was fun with a capital 'F'. I had recently jumped in at the deep end of the London flat-sharing life, and there, for the first time, I had to cook and fend for myself. I soon discovered my love of food, its preparation, and the fascination of different ingredients, spices and flavourings. This desire to taste, try and learn has never left me.

I was extremely fortunate in having as flatmates two Dutch girls who worked as cookery demonstrators for the Dutch Dairy Bureau in London. My father was the Consul for the Netherlands in Birmingham at that time, and part of his function was to promote Holland in his city. This brought with it trips by air to the Keukenhof, near Amsterdam, to see the bulbs and flower festivals in the local Birmingham parks, and cheese and wine evenings – which is how I met Anne-Marie Massalt and Elly Baum.

Some of the girls' perks from DDB (as they called the Bureau) were beautiful creamy Gouda and the waxy red-skinned Edam cheeses; also unsalted butter, crispy biscuits and various vegetables and other ingredients left over from their demonstrations. We even got the odd half bottle of Kirsch or Bols Genever Gin!

It was amazing how inventive we became with our meals, especially towards the end of the week when the money ran out. Hunger is a great teacher and Dutch cheese became the basis of many of our dishes. Long before pizzas became popular we made our own version with flaky pastry lining an oblong flan case and topped with layers of sliced Gouda, chopped tomatoes, chopped ham or bacon and literally anything else we had in the fridge – anchovies, pimentos, sweetcorn, olives, even garlic sausage. Popped into a hot oven until the pastry was golden and well risen, the filling cooked and bubbling, it was hot, crispy, filling and delicious. We used to eat it with a tossed green salad, chunks of French bread from the delicatessen around the corner, and a bottle of brutally chilled white 'plonk' – it was a banquet.

In the time following my marriage to Peter, I travelled frequently with him and we were entertained in homes and restaurants all over the world. I became fascinated by other cultures and tastes. Before long I started to compile my own recipe book, adding to my 'family' recipes many that were begged, borrowed, copied or freely given.

People, I concluded, tend to fall into two categories, those who are delighted to discuss the dishes they have prepared and take it as a compliment to be asked about the contents and the method used, and those who promise to let you have the recipe later – and then, somehow, always forget.

To the former I give my deep thanks, for they are the ones I remember with fondness every time I open a particular page in my book; the memories flood back and the meal tastes just that little bit more special.

Many of the recipes that you will find here are simple, quick and easy to prepare. Occasionally, if the evening demands it, I will produce a dish with something 'extra' to it, but as a busy mum with three children and a very hectic household, I prefer to leave the complicated cookery to the professional chefs and to glory in the perfection of it when I myself am out to dine.

HOME ENTERTAINING – ME AND MY KITCHEN

My kitchen is very much the centre of our home, a working kitchen, but toys tend to litter the floor and many's the time I've found a child curled up, thumb in mouth and fast asleep with one of the dogs on the rug against the comforting warmth of the double Aga.

Cooking on an Aga has meant that I have struggled a little with the recipes in this book, purely because the methods of cooking and timing are so different from a conventional gas or electric cooker. For my own purposes I have adopted a 'touch and tell' technique: if it looks done, I test it either with a finger or with a skewer, and if it needs another few minutes, I pop it back. It works well with the majority of things except for soufflés and certain cakes which sink if the oven door is opened. The electric/gas figures which accompany the recipes in the book are based on extensive tests which I have conducted or organized in the homes of many kind and patient friends. Rest assured, they *do* work!

I am an avid reader of cookery books old and new, and my desk, kitchen pinboard and even my handbags are full of cuttings of cookery articles that I have taken from a newspaper or magazine. Eventually I sit down and sort through them, putting the best aside to try on some unsuspecting guest.

Curiosity has taken me into some of the most humble kitchens and also into many of the top hotel kitchens in this country. Everywhere, I have met enthusiasm and kindness. Many a simple tip has been gleaned this way. Maybe my greatest regret is my lack of formal training in the early years. How much more simple it would have been, avoiding all those long painful hours of experimenting. Oh, to have known some of those professional short cuts!

CASUAL EVENINGS

Dinner parties in the Alliss household tend to be either formal silver-and-candle affairs or unsophisticated breakfast-room get-togethers. Casual nights, when friends drop in for a drink and stay for supper, mean the simplest of fare. Maybe a bowl of piping hot home-made soup to start, or pâté, quickly defrosted, with crunchy bread and chunks of crispy fennel. Sometimes no starter, just a main course rounded off with fresh fruit and cheese.

One of my favourites is pasta, cooked in lots of salted boiling water and then tossed in cream, grated Gruyère cheese, lots of chopped fresh herbs from the garden and masses of freshly ground black pepper. Scrummy, especially when followed by a tossed crisp Iceberg Salad.

Chicken Suprême is another quick favourite: minutes to defrost and then the breasts stuffed with Gruyère cheese, butter and freshly chopped parsley, brushed with melted butter and secured with a cocktail stick and roasted for about 35 minutes. The compliments will fly when these succulent little golden parcels reach the table.

I think I love those casual evenings the best. The conversation sparkles and I find that our guests gravitate into the kitchen to perch on the Aga, and on stools or kitchen worktops, glass in hand, in order to chat and keep me company while I sort out the meal.

FORMAL EVENINGS

These take more planning. Part of the fun is balancing guests to complement each other – a lesson I learnt painfully when we invited some acquaintances to dine with some distinguished French visitors who were staying with us. One English 'friend' referred loudly to 'the Froggies' all through dinner and I developed an incessant nervous chat to try and prevent the French people from overhearing his remarks.

I well remember, too, being a young bride in Yorkshire and having good friends to stay who were Jewish. I ordered a huge shoulder of pork from my butchers for Sunday lunch. Then, while we were out to dine at the local inn on Saturday evening and were all studying the menu, the wife remarked casually that they were quite orthodox in their eating habits. I quietly died. There followed a hasty 'Excuse me' and a desperate plea to the hotel owner: 'Please sell me a couple of chickens!' Luckily for me, he did!

Table setting, too, plays a major part in formal dining. The day before the party, I decide on a colour scheme and organize the table flowers! I like arrangements that are both long and low enough not to obscure anyone's vision; many's the time I've sat at a table hearing the voice but only seeing the foliage.

I tend to favour soft colours, the greens, greys and silvers of garden ferns, leaves and plants; shades of pink from palest blush to deep fuschia, and, favourite of all, pure white and cream. The silver cutlery gleams, and crystal candelabras are set in place with complementary candles; the highly polished table glows and it almost seems a shame to spoil it by serving the meal.

Simple garden flowers can be most effective, too, as table decorations – closely packed delicate primroses and pale green ivy, or asparagus fern. Try an oasis foam ball stuck onto a pin base which itself is attached to a glass plate. Cover the ball with tiny wild flowers or spring flowers until there is not an inch of foam to be seen, and then cover the plate with soft green garden moss. Dampened, it will keep the flowers and foam moist and fresh and it is devastatingly effective.

In winter, rosy Chilean Red Delicious apples, polished to a high gloss and placed one in front of each guest, are novel and inexpensive. Cut a slice into the top of each apple and pop in a place card. In the centre of the table, pile a glass bowl high with more polished apples and tiny sprigs of silvery eucalyptus slipped into the gaps. Guaranteed to draw compliments.

I'm not fond of overhead lighting, preferring several table lamps and their subdued hues. I think all women from twenty to eighty prefer soft light, and somehow the conversation flows in the intimate atmosphere that soft light creates.

During our years of travelling we have made a habit of collecting unusual table bits and pieces, such as intricately carved ivory condiments from Japan, cleverly found by my husband; tiny white porcelain angels that grace the Christmas table, three-inch high painted wooden candle ladies from Antigua, in glowing colours, with candles to match, and white pottery daisies from Spain, set in a circle around a huge shallow bowl of spring violets, arresting in their simplicity, their colour accentuated by violet linen napkins.

I make a point of visiting the local pottery or craft shops in any country I visit, and many of my favourite pieces have come from the most unlikely shops. Maybe a tin shack on a Caribbean island. Among my treasures are some tiny individual 'Wee Willie Winkie' candle-holders I found in Scotland; I place one by each guest and every face glows in the soft subtle light they throw.

KEEP IT FRESH

I gave up using a freezer – as an aid to entertaining, that is – some while ago. I use mine now purely for bread, meat, and sausage rolls and fish fingers etc., for the children. I have tried pre-cooking food for a dinner party and freezing it the week before but somehow it feels like cheating to me and I never honestly think it tastes as good as freshly prepared food. I am fanatical about freshness and like to pick my vegetables on the morning of a dinner party – we are blessed with marvellous pick-your-own fruit and vegetable farms in our area. I love to find unexpected combinations of textures and ingredients, and I still use good fresh butter and cream in the dishes that call for them.

So, simply, entertaining should be fun – for you and your guests. Do as much as possible before the guests arrive and never try to do anything too ambitious. *Never* try out a new recipe on the day, and above all don't panic if things go wrong. A calm smiling face, and another glass of wine, and the worst problem can be overcome.

CHAPTER TWO

SWITZERLAND AND GERMANY

BUT BACK TO THE BEGINNING! As a young girl I was sent by my father to Lausanne University in Switzerland to improve my French and to acquire (hopefully) a degree, some poise and a little *savoir-faire*!

Looking back, it was a magical time in my life. I was fresh out of school, full of optimism, and free from parental control for the very first time. I left England determined to enjoy every minute of my stay.

How uncomplicated life was then. We had picnics by the side of Lake Léman, the lakeside walk ablaze with magnolia trees so heavy with their creamy white blossoms, they looked for all the world like rows of white crinolined ladies curtseying low to the water. Warm summer evenings and barbecues by the waterside. The fires glowed, and when the food was eaten we were ready for a sing-song and students from all over the place contributed songs in their own language; there was a glorious sense of unity amongst us all.

By day we worked hard, and after several months I experienced the joy of realizing that I could now converse sensibly and fluently with people I met around town.

Classes at the University started at 8.30 am, and to get there I had to climb some 300 stone steps to the Faculté des Lettres. Up and down, four times a day; I would have been pencil-slim had I not discovered Swiss chocolate.

In the winter months we could be found, between classes, in one of the many tempting patisseries, hands cupped around huge bowls of steaming hot chocolate with dollops of thick cream on top, all talking at once in French, German, English, Italian and Spanish.

I still love the Swiss patisseries, so different from our own cake shops. I love their rich fruit flans, succulent Swiss Wähe, crisp and golden and filled with delicate slices of overlapping crescents of apple. Flans of tiny sweet/sour Morello cherries and plum flans, my favourite, made with the shortest of shortcrust pastry, filled with those small purple plums called Zwetschen, and a rich custard poured over the top when nearly cooked – end result, mouthwateringly good. There were fluffy cheesecakes, crispy light biscuits and chocolate cakes that defy description.

Swiss chocolate is, in some people's eyes, the best in the world, and it was from this period in my life that my collection of chocolate recipes began: **Chocolate Roulades, Nègre en Chemise, Chocolate Chestnut Cream**, etc. I have rarely met a man or a child who does not like chocolate desserts. One of my children's favourites, for lunch on a cold winter's day, is the old-fashioned steamed chocolate pud with lots of chocolate chips stirred into the mixture before cooking, with chocolate sauce and thick dairy cream. Well worth getting fat for!

I stayed for the first eight months in Lausanne in the Pension Cuénoud. It waas run by two lovely old ladies, Madame Cuénoud and her sister Madame Singey. They were a delightful pair, and spoiled me terribly as I was the only girl lodger staying with them (there were six boys). They were also convinced that I did not eat enough. As I was then 8½ stone and increasing rapidly I can only think they had a Rubens-tinted view of what young girls should look like.

The apartment was in an old block on the edge of town, full of lovely old furniture, highly polished floors which gleamed in the sun and smelt of lavender. The rooms were spacious and had spotless snowy white linen and duvets that were thrown across the balcony each day to air. In the mornings it looked as if half the fluffy clouds from the mountain tops had dropped down into the valley and town below; in the sunshine and clean air everything sparkled.

The greatest shock to any system in those first weeks was the discovery that cold water was the order of the day – and every day, except Friday, which was bath night! Nobody ever missed bath night; it was the one evening we never accepted invitations, it was our only chance for a long soak and to wash our hair. Even then people banged on the door after half an hour and I was always extremely grateful that there was only one female lodger in the house for I automatically went first.

I remember, about six months after my arrival, I decided to change the colour of my hair. It was a very daring thing to do in those days and certainly not something I would have risked at home under my father's stern eye. Jet black, I thought, raising visions of Anne of Green Gables and 'Diana' of the magnolia skin and raven's-wing hair. 'Black Tulip', it said on the label, which sounded good to me. But, horror of horrors, the end result was a deep, almost fuchsia red! I spent a week washing my hair in freezing water every morning and every evening to get the worst of it out, and it was months before the rest of the Pension stopped called me 'La Radis' – the radish!

Mealtimes at the Pension were prompt. The gong for lunch went at 12.30 and the conversations were lively and sometimes quite heated as we discussed the morning's classes. We sat round a large circular table and it was here at Mme Cuénoud's that I first had Pis-en-lit Salad: delicious dandelion leaves, dark and slightly bitter with chopped hard-boiled egg; and **Swiss Onion Tart**, amazingly good with crispy pastry and masses of thick creamy onion filling – my own version of Swiss Onion Tart is as near to this as I can get. There was a wonderful apple dish as well. Apples were cut into thick crescents and fried in unsalted butter, lemon juice and sugar in a heavy-bottomed pan until soft, flamed with Calvados and carried to the table still alight; the sauce was rich and thick in the pan and there was never a spoonful left.

Switzerland taught me to love cheese and also to cook with it. There were Swiss Fondues made with Gruyère and Kirsch, eaten with chunks of French bread dipped into the boiling cheesy mixture. And Gougères, as light as a feather and filled with a savoury cream-cheese mixture. And grated Gruyère cheese and chopped parsley, mixed together in equal quantities and sprinkled over soup when serving or as a topping for vegetables, or indeed, any savoury dish.

Raclette was another favourite, sometimes eaten high in the mountains after a hard day's skiing. An oval-shaped cheese is held over an open fire and as it melts lovely soft slices are scraped off onto plates grasped in outstretched hands. To go with it we drank local beer and ate crusty French bread and salad. Sitting by the log fire, tired but exhilarated after the day's exercise, the stories came thick and fast – surely they couldn't all have been true?!!

My first summer there, I took a holiday job in the mountain village of Montrâchet, looking after the daughter of the local hotelier and his wife. The child, Mimi, aged three, was not easy; an only child and somewhat spoiled, she resented a stranger taking her away from Mummy. But the days passed in the peaceful countryside, walking, collecting wild flowers and just wandering in the warm sunshine around the village, talking to the locals. In the early evening, with Mimi washed, fed and sung to sleep (amazing how effective English lullabies proved to be), I was free to go to the dairy, some three-quarters of a mile away, to fetch the Gruyère and cream for the hotel's evening trade. Wandering home in the twilight with just the cowbells and the birds winging back to their nests for company, the mountains towering, snow-topped above me and the air calm and still, they were possibly the most peaceful times I have ever known.

It was here in the kitchens, deep in the heart of the hotel, that I learnt to eat cheese as an appetizer, cut into thin strips and dunked into French mustard, always accompanied by a glass of chilled local white wine. The Chef was a huge jovial man who teased me unmercifully and kept telling me that the only way to become fluent in French was to sleep with a Frenchman. As I was not fluent enough to produce a quick reply I spent a lot of time tongue-tied and as flushed as the red cherries which stood in bowls on the long pine kitchen table.

Mealtimes, for us, were always around 10.00 pm after the Chef had finished with the restaurant clientèle. The wine flowed, and we sat around the table in eager anticipation of the good things to come. He never disappointed us, serving wafer-thin slices of calves' liver flashed in butter and rosemary and slices of fresh local peaches, dropped at the last minute in the foaming butter. Veal Escallops, pan-fried in butter, with mushrooms and cream. Veal Noisettes, small round and tender, cooked in apple, butter and Calvados. Tender steaks, simply done with garlic and parsley, accompanied by huge local field mushrooms or some of the many varied *cèpes* to be found in the area and much sought after by the locals. Chicken, stuffed with goat's cheese, herbs and parsley or casseroled with fennel and tomato paste with juniper berries – and always a huge, huge bowl of salad in the centre of the table with every mixture of leaves available and every night a different dressing. Blue cheese; vinaigrette; lemon, honey and yoghurt; walnut oil and French wine vinegar, or, my favourite, a delicious dressing made from creamy milk, walnut oil and lemon juice that I have been trying to copy ever since! This, plus the inevitable platefuls of crispy golden *pommes frites* served with every meal, and batons of crusty French bread for all to help themselves to, and plenty of local wine. Desserts tended to be whatever fruit was available – huge peaches, firm and downy with an apricot hue, deep red cherries and always grapes in abundance to eat with the local cheese. I was sad to say goodbye at the end of my six-week stay.

Then my days at Lausanne came slowly to an end and it was

home again to my parents. However, I found I had developed a travel bug, an urge to see another country and learn another language. So, after a short spell teaching by day at the local kindergarten, and cramming German by night, within six months I was off again, this time to Wuppertal, near Düsseldorf in West Germany.

The ensuing months were, unlike Switzerland, not the happiest of times. I went there mainly to go to school, staying with a family as a *Haustochter* (house daughter). In return for my board and lodging, I was to teach French and English to the four children of the household. Frau Fudikar was 5 ft 10 in tall, weighed easily 14 stone and had a booming voice that went with her clipped masculine hairstyle. The eldest daughter, Marion, was two years younger than me, topped me by six inches and three stone and was a smaller replica of her mother. Gabriella, aged 14, was quiet and studious and I related better to her than the others, simply because she listened to me. Then came Sybilla, aged 10, and Dietrich, aged 7 – the 'Terrible Twosome'! Herr Fudikar was tiny, only 5 ft 2 in, thin and wiry, but he ruled the household with a rod of iron. Far worse than his bossiness, however, was his habit of sneaking up on me when I went to feed the Doberman dog by the broom cupboard under the stairs! I lived in fear that one day he would actually succeed in his efforts to open the door and push me through. Herr Fudikar was definitely a dirty old man, but somehow I always escaped.

Lunch, unfailingly, was a time of mental torture. On the dot of 12.30 the gong went and we stood for grace. Then came the third-degree grilling of the children on that day's schooling and their results, and heaven help the child, usually Sybilla, who managed no higher than a B-minus. Every mealtime there were pale faces and tears, and it was harassing for everyone below the rank of parent, me included. I never knew when the father might shoot me some question about English history or French, and then chastise me when I either didn't know or didn't understand! When lunch was at last finished, he would adjourn to his sitting room, which was strictly forbidden to the children and me. There he would eat the peach tarts I had prepared that morning, drink his coffee and sleep until it was time to go back to his clothing factory.

I had nightmares about those *Pfirsichtorten* (peach tarts). Each morning I had to prepare two small individual sponge cakes, pop one tinned peach half in each, thicken a little of the juice with cornflour and when cool coat the peaches with the sauce. If the sponge bases did not turn out just right, I had to start all over again.

Shortly after arriving in the household I made the mistake of saying that I could sew. Suddenly two bolts of brushed cotton material appeared with the request – 'Bitte!' – that I should make the children some pyjamas. Panic! I'd never made a pair before, and really hadn't much of a clue. However, there was a bonus in that the room in which the sewing maching was situated was large, comfortable, sunny and high up on the third floor, where I could escape to sew in peace with my radio and the English news on the World Service.

In the evenings I often went out for coffee with an English girl, Sue, whom I had met at my school there. She lived with a family in the next road. The problem with those visits was getting back into the house unnoticed. Frau Fudikar would inevitably be sitting by herself in the kitchen drinking schnapps, her husband having retired as he disapproved of alcohol. No matter how quietly I let myself in through the front door she always heard the key and as I tiptoed past she would insist that I should have a small glassful to keep her company before going to bed. I became adept at tipping it into any available bowl, plant or milk jug, but just occasionally I'd actually have to drink it, a whole tumblerful of neat schnapps! To this day I shudder at the memory and never touch gin, vodka or schnapps!

But my memories of Germany are not all bad. I loved their marvellous *pommes frites* stands in the streets where you could buy bags of thin crispy chips with creamy mayonnaise, or hot dogs straight from the boiling water vats popped into a soft roll with German mustard. We used to buy them on our way back from the cinema or school, and it became quite a social gathering when several of us students stopped to buy and talk. Sauerkraut became a favourite; hot-spiced red cabbage, such as you will find in my recipe with apple and onion. Mutton, which we often ate with redcurrants, was delicious, and whole fish, steamed and eaten with a marvellous mayonnaise sauce full of chopped gherkins. And always salads, at every meal.

The family's kindly housekeeper, Frau Hein, and her husband befriended me. They lived in a self-contained flat on the fourth floor, up in the attics, and I often escaped to the tranquillity of their rooms. To get there after three flights of stairs, one had to go through the attics, and this route always reduced me to helpless laughter because the family underwear used to be hung over the roof beams to dry. It was there I discovered that Herr Fudikar wore thick woollen all-in-ones from his neck to his toes. Coming, as I did, from a very spartan English household, I did find them enormously funny. This was, remember, long before Princess Di and her confessed fondness for thermals. To me, Herr Fudikar's undergarments were very unromantic, especially in view of his designs on me.

SWITZERLAND AND GERMANY

Wuppertal is famous for its *Schwebebahn*, an overhead suspension railway, rather like our underground system but running above the town instead of below. The only railway of its kind, it was quick and an enormously efficient way of getting from one end of the town to the other. It was also famous for its Army troops, largely British, who were stationed there. I was friendly with a German officer, Joseph, who rescued me occasionally from my school work and took me to the Officers' Mess and to dinner dances. It was very different from my own experiences of Army life, gained because of my father, and I found it both fascinating and very enjoyable. I also met, at school, a man called Tom Gilbey, who had a burning desire to design men's clothes. Today when I look in the newspapers I often see that name, now famous, and wonder if it is indeed the same Tom!

I stayed in Germany for 12 months, acquired fluent German, a lot of friends, and several more recipes for my collection! Then, once more, it was time to head for home, and a job.

CHAPTER THREE

FAMILY COOKS
AND A
YEAR IN STRATFORD

MY TRAVELS TEMPORARILY OVER, back I went to my parents' comfortable home on the outskirts of Birmingham for a rest – and to lose weight – before deciding on the next move.

My father was a lawyer, well known and loved by many. A man with enormous energy and time for everyone and everything. He was a man of varied interests – and maybe in this we were alike, sharing a desire to do and not to sit. He taught me to try to understand and appreciate people from all walks of life, to have a sense of humour and a sense of the ridiculous when things were not going well.

He came from a staunch Baptist background. His father (my Grandfather Grey) was also a lawyer and a former Lord Mayor of Birmingham, and he too sat on the local bench, as did my father and as I do today. A strict teetotaller, my grandfather strongly disapproved of my father's seemingly flippant outlook on life during his Oxford student days, and what was worse, his taste for alcohol. Drink was strictly forbidden in the household, so much so that my father's eldest sister had to suffer a dry wedding reception at Birmingham Town hall. Father's reputation was further tarnished when he and several undergraduate friends laced the fruit juice with brandy from their hip flasks! Grandmama tried to soften things between her husband and her beloved only son, but at the end of World War II, when my father came home with the rank of Captain and was now also responsible for a wife and two tiny babies, he was offered only a minor partnership in the family law firm. He decided to leave and set up on his own.

He and a colleague, David Dawkins, then founded a practice that was to prove a highly successful partnership and lasted until my father's death in 1983.

In peacetime my father was a colonel in the Territorials. He loved the Army life and I suspect would have enjoyed being a Regular. However, my own feelings are that he had the best of both worlds and we benefited from his wealth of experience.

For me, as a child, and for my sister Sally, who is two years older than me, Christmas parties were magical times. The Drill Hall at Walsall was transformed for the occasion, and when Father Christmas appeared from the wide stone chimney, a sack full of presents over each shoulder we were speechless with pleasure. The fact that Santa bore more than a passing resemblance to the Duty Sergeant never crossed our minds.

When I was older, I had the excitement of attending my first Regimental Ball. The uniform 'Blues' of the officers, the billowing gowns of the ladies, the medals sparkling on proud chests, spurs jangling and all those handsome young subalterns dancing attendance on the Colonel's daughters! No wonder I grew up to be such a romantic. Breakfast at three in the morning and carriages at four, and oh! the memories. Of a distinguished General clinging to the lamp-post and earnestly asking it the way home. Of my father dancing the Gay Gordons with me – he was an enthusiastic but rotten dancer, and he loved every minute of it; so did I, bruised toes and all. Of stolen kisses and falling in love for at least two weeks afterwards. Of the oysters that made me so ill, I wanted to die. Of brass bands, of marching music and the haunting sound of the 'Last Post' being played in total silence, the parading of the regimental colours and the sheer marvellous tradition and Englishness of it all.

My father died, after a short illness, four weeks after our youngest son was born. I still miss him dreadfully and I hope that little Henry has inherited some of his grandfather's great qualities.

I am, I suppose, a Brummie, as I was born in Queen Elizabeth Hospital, some twelve miles from the city centre. I was educated privately at Edgbaston High School. I quite enjoyed school but only, I think, because my sister did not, and was always in trouble, while I, brat that I was, was a bit of a goodie-goodie, careful to do and say the right things at the right times. With hindsight I cannot for the life of me see why my sister cared so much for me, but she did and was always leaping to my defence if needed.

We had a succession of nannies, some remembered, some not, and life seemed pleasant and always sunny to us. I remember the year I was ten and the garden was full of tiny frogs. Sally and I caught some, painted them garish colours with water paints and then chased the then nanny with them. She was petrified by anything that moved (by us too, I suspect!). We cornered her in the garden loo and kept her there for over an hour by pushing little frogs through the gap under the door. When our mother finally came to her rescue, the nanny was stiff with fright, and mother was furious with us for laughing!

I remember scrumping apples from the next-door neighbour's garden. Theirs looked redder than ours. It was years before I found out that the policeman who frogmarched us back home, ashamed and penitent, and lectured us on pinching apples, was a great family friend! That day we learnt a very good lesson on how to respect the law and other people's belongings!

My mother is a good cook and many of my recipes are old and trusted family ones, such as **Chicken Liver Pâté** which I make frequently. I cook it in large quantities, swear like a seaman when I am up to my elbows in bloody livers and garlic, but it is always worthwhile in the end when I proudly survey the rows of filled pâté dishes sealed with butter, warm and fragrant – and it freezes beautifully.

My **Christmas Cake** is another family recipe. Well tried and tested, it always produces a moist rich cake. I've added bits over the years and am now very pleased with the result. It doesn't need to be made many months in advance (I make mine in October), wrap it in lots of greaseproof paper and then foil; the marzipan goes on about ten days before Christmas and I ice it about two days before serving.

Each Christmas when I was a child my maternal grandmother (Grandmother Trimmingham) spent the holiday with us. Father and I always fetched her from her home early on Christmas Eve, collecting two turkeys from Walsall Territorial Army Barracks at the same time. One turkey was for us, the other for Grey Gables, a home for elderly ladies in Birmingham which had been founded by Grandfather Grey. First we went to the home to deliver their turkey to Matron. There would be a large sherry for Father, an orange juice for me, and several whiskery kisses from the old ladies, and then back we went to our house in Edgbaston to prepare and stuff the turkey, and decorate the tree.

I well remember the year the turkeys arrived unplucked and undrawn. Horror of horrors! My mother threw a fit of the vapours and retired. Sally, aged 12, went an interesting shade of green and retired, and my grandmother and I, aged 10, coped. We laid out sheet after sheet of newspaper, my father found some pliers to pull out the leg sinews, and we had huge bags to stuff the feathers into. But, oh, the smell! That and the sight of Grannie's arm up to the elbow drawing out the entrails will stay with me for the rest of my days. And how we laughed in between fits of sneezing brought on by all the free-flying feathers. The good thing about that experience was that I have never since been squeamish about preparing fish or game in my own kitchen!

As youngsters, Sally and I were fortunate in having a much-loved great aunt who lived in Knock, Northern Ireland. Long before the present troubles we spent many happy weeks with her during our holidays. We travelled on the overnight ferry from Liverpool to Belfast Docks. Mother always fondly believed we were tucked up in our cabin asleep, but little did she know that we spent most of the night clinging to the rails and walking the decks, shrieking with fear every time the ship rolled, as it frequently did in the rough and turbulent Irish Sea. It was such an adventure, as we left Liverpool, to watch the lights from the dockside fading away behind us, and to look for the lights of Douglas on the Isle of Man, then seeing just the blackness of the inky dark sea and hearing the noise of the engines and the waves rushing past. Wide-eyed, we watched our progress steaming up the wide Belfast Lough in the early hours, everything clear and sparkling in the morning dew with nothing but the odd fishing trawler or lazily moving coal barge for company.

Aunt Nan and Uncle George lived on the outskirts of Belfast. She was an avid golfer and Lady Captain at Belvoir Golf Club. They were such a happy couple, and I remember my visits with great fondness and can, to this day, recall the aroma in her kitchen when it was time for tea. The freshly baked breads of bran, fruit, soda and granary, the salty, creamy butter, the sizzling ham and eggs, the teapot sitting in the hearth with its old iron fender, and me, curled up in the warm on the floor beside the dog.

It was Aunt Nan who first introduced me to golf. I don't think, even in those days, I was a budding Curtis Cup player, but I remember I enjoyed it! We had homely, long, lazy days sightseeing and shopping in Belfast, going on day trips to Dublin or to the coast. I often think I could retire to Ireland. I love the gentle pace, the softness of the countryside with the hills shrouded in mist and the muted colours of the heathers and gorse. I love the lilting speech, the generous hospitality, the humour and the friendliness of the people.

Years after my girlhood visits, my husband went on a business trip from Belfast to Dublin in the company of a lovely Irishman called

Jim Fitzgibbon. They somehow lost three days and Peter ended up buying three acres of land high above Bantry Bay. To this very day he remembers little between the first 'Let's just stop awhile, you must meet this wee friend', and turning up in Dublin two days later. It was quite a shock when, after several months had passed, the deeds of the land and the bill arrived.

In 1979, one glorious Autumn weekend, we went to look at our land. Perched high above the bay on the south-west tip of Ireland, overlooking romantic Garnish Island which is subtropical and ablaze with plants and exotic vegetation, and Whiddy Island, a complete contrast with its modern trappings of oil tankers, and fuelling storage facilities. Our land sits in lonely splendour, breathtaking in its magnificence, high above the village up a dirt track, with just the wheeling seagulls for company, the sunsets glowing in brilliant colours and the winds whispering through the glorious heather.

We applied for, and got, planning permission, put in the footings and there we stopped. How does anyone get a lorry up a two foot wide dirt track some hundreds of feet in the air? But I would still love to build a sprawling slate bungalow, long and low with windows facing south or west – maybe one day!

We stayed in a pale pink-washed Georgian mansion, newly converted into a hotel. Sparkling, crisp, sunny days gave way to cooler evenings spent in front of a roaring fire with lots of Irish hospitality. By day we drove lazily round the Ring of Kerry, pausing frequently to take gulps of clear fresh air and admire the view. On Irish roads, lazily is the only way to go, as the ruts and holes make any kind of speed impossible! We dropped into Waterford to see Colm O'Connor, Deputy Chairman of Waterford Crystal and an old friend. On the day we chose to go, the workers came out on strike and the place was in silent chaos! Lots of cheers from mad-keen golfers greeted us. Then a brave few, amid catcalls and further cheers, demonstrated to us the art of glass blowing.

Our evenings in Ireland were relaxed, and a superb meal inevitably ended with piping hot Gaelic Coffee. Our genial host said it should be made as follows:

Put a heaped teaspoon of sugar into the bottom of a large, warmed balloon wine glass. Stir in a good measure of whiskey (Irish, of course!) and then fill to within 1 inch of the brim with hot, strong, fresh black coffee. Hold a dessertspoon over the coffee and carefully pour double cream over the back of the spoon – as much as you like – and serve at once!

FAMILY COOKS AND A YEAR IN STRATFORD

In Switzerland we used to drink a mixture of equal parts coffee and hot chocolate, sometimes laced with a little brandy and cream. After this Irish holiday, I looked up several coffee recipes and adapted some of my own.

The children love Coffee Milk Shakes, which I make by dissolving 2 teaspoons of instant coffee and 1 teaspoon of sugar in a tablespoon of hot water. Put about ¼ pt (150 ml) ice-cold creamy milk into the blender, add the coffee and three good scoops of vanilla ice cream. Blend and pour into tall glasses. It is delicious and is equally good made with drinking chocolate.

Petit Pots de Crème au Café is another favourite with us. I found the recipe for this in a super little book popped into my Christmas stocking. It is easy to make, being a variation on **Crème Brûlée**; we like our Pots served very chilled with fresh strawberries. Then there is **Coffee and Walnut Cake**, another pound-adding cake. Did you know, by the way, that in Turkey, when a Turkish man asked a father for his daughter's hand in marriage, he had to promise him that his bride would never go short of coffee. If she did, it was legitimate grounds for divorce.

But back to life in our family, and in particular, my sister Sally. Taller than me, blonde, green-eyed, she and I are in many ways unalike, but I think we share our fiercely independent streak (some may call it stubborn) and a love of travelling; we are also very good friends. Sally is a good cook with a preference for the more exotic dishes. She loves hot spices with unpronounceable names for which she scours the local delicatessens. Living in London, as she does, she is never short on variety.

She has a wicked sense of of humour and many's the time I have opened the morning's post to find just a cartoon cut out and stuck onto a blank piece of paper, vastly appropriate to whatever situation or row is current in our family and guaranteed to reduce me to helpless laughter! Like the one she sent me when we had a geriatric aunt who wore a wig because she had gone bald – she would not survive the shock, she said, if the wig were to be removed. Through the post came a cutting about a man who had invented a special safety bed for geriatric patients in case of fire. When the alarm bell went, the bed tilted upwards, the window opened automatically and the patient was shot head-first through the window onto a chute and down into the garden. Did he, Sally wondered, have a suggestion for saving all these lovely old dears from dying of a heart attack in the process?

Another classic was the cutting that arrived a few days after my small son, playing Batman,leapt off a stone wall and badly sprained his ankle. I had told her the story over the telephone, including my child's sorrowful cry of 'Why can't I fly like Batman, Mummy?' Entitled 'Batman's Caper in Bedroom', the story was about a respectable man living in the Australian suburb of St Lucia near Brisbane. Each evening the man, a well-dressed local businessman, arrived home, picked up the milk on the doorstep and went inside. When full bottles were left outside for two days in a row, worried neighbours called the police. They walked in through the unlocked front door to find the man's naked wife chained to a bed, a hanky tied over her mouth. Pinned beneath a toppled wardrobe, with a broken leg, was her amorous husband dressed in a skintight Batman suit. 'Was this,' Sally wrote, 'shades of things to come?' So that's the kind of family I belong to!

Having arrived home from Germany, I decided I would quite like to fly. The glamour of travel, of far-away places and my love of meeting people made an airline an obvious choice, so off I went to BOAC, Pan-Am and a few others. To my great delight, both Pan-Am and BOAC accepted me with the proviso that, as I was under their minimum age, for six months I would have to do something useful which involved people (the choice was mine), and also lose half a stone in weight!

Little did I know then that neither airline was to have the pleasure of employing me, for when I eventually left Stratford-upon-Avon Hospital, where I went to do my 'people service', the desire to fly had gone and new opportunities had opened up.

But at the beginning of that phase in my life I found myself one day, cloak in hand, nervously accepting to be an Auxiliary Nurse under Matron, Miss Mortell, and moving in with my favourite Aunt Jean and her husband and cousins who live at Bearley, some four miles north of Stratford. They were gloriously happy days, twelve months of fun, tears of both misery and laughter, of pink-faced embarrassment while doing my first male bed-bath, of bravado and sheer fatigue coupled with an enormous sense of achievement.

I started on the female medical ward with a blonde girl called Jane. She was fair and I was dark, and we quickly got the nickname 'The Terrible Twins' and became firm friends. Jane, like me, was doing a year for the experience, but she was then going on to St Barts in London to take a full training course; for both of us this year was going to be a giggle. I don't think either of us realized how hard we were going to be worked: auxiliary nurses get little sympathy and most of the dirty work is thrown at them.

FAMILY COOKS AND A YEAR IN STRATFORD

The hospital, on the north side of Stratford, was an old Victorian building with a block of six long wards, reminiscent of nissen huts, joined by a long covered walkway. Each ward had, I think, 24 beds, 12 a side, and to get to this block from the main building one had to walk across a driveway, which on Wednesdays was the road leading to the cattle market and therefore full of sheep and cattle lorries.

After my first three days I phoned my mother in tears. My feet were blistered, I told her, my back ached and my hands were red raw from scrubbing bed pans – no automatic sterilizers in those days! There must be more to life than this, I remember saying, nothing but rubbing bottoms and bedpans!

Worse was to come. At the beginning of my second week a farmer's wife was admitted as an emergency, with a coronary. After the doctors had left, I was told to sit with her and to press the emergency bell if her condition changed. Changed! Within twenty minutes she suddenly turned purple, choked and died within the space of five seconds before my frantic pressing on the bell could summon help. The patient had had a second massive heart attack; no-one could have done anything, but it was my first experience of death and it was a very sobering one. I was told to assist with the 'laying-out' and then to take her to the mortuary. I remember the Staff Nurse's sympathetic eyes as she performed the necessary duties and my stomach heaved. By the end of that day I had grown up considerably and learnt my first real lesson in life – not to panic in emergencies and to face death.

From this shaky start I never looked back. I found I loved the responsibility of nursing, the strong sense of unity among the staff, the sheer pleasure of talking and often reassuring patients, and the humour to be found in so many situations. Patients having to undergo surgery were nearly always joking and cheerful, hiding their aches and pains until their dearly beloveds arrived at visiting time. Jane and I were the butt of many of their jokes: lengths of cotton stretched between the beds to trip us up when carrying bed bottles; red paint on their bandages and a panicked 'Look nurse, I'm bleeding!' – enough to send us racing for 'Staff' and a lecture on naivety when she had investigated. Rock-bun fights with the buns flying like missiles across the ward, and Jane and I caught helplessly in the line of fire. Sister was furious. And I lost track of how many times I got locked in the bathroom! The nurses were always starving – but I remember there were marvellous dishes of milk pudding each day on the meal trolleys. They were strictly forbidden to the staff, nevertheless we always managed a quick bowlful behind the sluice doors in company with the bedpans. Very hygienic, on reflection!

During this time, I lived with my relations in their beautiful Tudor house on the edge of Bearley village. Low ceilings with heavy oak beams to crack your forehead if you didn't quickly learn to duck, and lattice windows with tiny panes that rattled in the rain and wind and glistened in the sunshine. The house overlooked sloping meadows, the village pond on one side, the village church on the other. It was a peaceful, off-the-track spot, ideal for walking or for just sitting dreaming on top of the five-barred gate.

Aunt Jean was trained as a professional cook in Edinburgh. She cooked for the troops during the war and was a joy to watch working, either for us and the evening meal, or for the many dinner parties she gave. I used to play first mate, helping, learning and clearing up, and I loved it. The kitchen was small, with uneven stone floors and a low ceiling hung with shining copper-bottomed pans. Aunt Jean had a minimal work surface, and an old solid-fuel Aga to cook on, yet I never saw her flustered, short of space or in disarray.

From her I learnt to keep a soup pan. Every scrap of leftover food was used up in this way, with the addition of lentils and good home-made stock, and it meant that there was always a bowlful of hot nourishing soup available to warm our tummies and cold hands.

Aunt Jean also taught me to bone chicken. I watched in wide-eyed amazement for the first time, and after many hours of practice managed to do in twenty minutes what she achieved in about seven. My recipe for **Lemon Chicken** came from her, and that for the delicious **Coeur à la Crème**, little heart-shaped moulds of a cheese mixture accompanied by a bowlful of the fresh raspberries or strawberries that grew in the garden in abundance alongside the vegetables.

And so the months rolled by and suddenly it was spring and time to move on. The desire to fly had gone, for I was now engaged to a boy I had known since childhood. Instead of going to one of the airlines I went for an interview with Gallahers. I got the job, moved to London, and within weeks my engagement was over. A few months later, I met my husband to be.

CHAPTER FOUR

YORKSHIRE IN THE SEVENTIES

IN 1970, AFTER MANY DIFFICULT months while Peter finalized his divorce and went through the inevitable heartache this causes, we moved to North Leeds, married at last, and set up our first home together. The ten years we spent in Yorkshire were to be very happy: three of our four children were born there, including Victoria who was severely mentally handicapped and whom we sadly lost five years ago.

We had our ups and downs – many more ups than downs – and I learnt an immeasurable amount from the marvellously close-knit Jewish community which took us to their hearts, welcomed us into their homes and shared their traditions with us.

We moved in on 5 November 1970. Peter had accepted a job at Moor Allerton Golf Club, and on the day we arrived the head green-keeper, Colin Geddes, had organized a Bonfire Party for his staff and we joined them. So, after a day of furniture vans and carpet fitters we ended up, tired and dirty, cooking potatoes in the fire, eating parkin and downing hot wine. The shock of the night was yet to come! Later that evening, sitting on the floor in the drawing room discussing the day amid a heap of packing cases, the room suddenly became alive – with mice!

On closer inspection they were tiny field voles, attracted by the warmth of the newly installed central heating – and they were every-where. As fast as we caught one, another ran across the floor. I remember going hysterically to bed as they scampered up the curtains next to us and my husband calmly saying, 'Don't worry, they've never been known to bite!'

Our house was perched beside the 17th fairway, high above the clubhouse. The view was spectacular but the wind hit us head-on – and there was nothing for 40 miles to stop it. I broke my heart over the garden, fondly picturing lilac, deliphiniums and hollyhocks, but nothing survived the dreaded wind. Eventually sense prevailed and we planted hardy trees and shrubs which now, some 17 years later, are mature and colourful.

In Leeds, I learnt an awful lot about traditional Jewish food. During the first two weeks a respected elder of the Jewish community, Doddy Aber, arrived on the doorstep to bid us welcome, with a dish of smoked herring and a mezuzzah. The first we ate – it was spiced, creamy and very different. The second was not for eating, but to us Christians represented a great compliment: the mezuzzah is the tiny symbol which is pinned outside Jewish homes to safeguard them, and we treasured ours. Indeed, when we left Yorkshire we brought it with us and it is now fixed to our present front door.

We learnt to eat bagels, piping hot from the oven, collected early on Sunday morning when the Jewish Sabbath was over and the bakers were back in business. Split, buttered and eaten with lashings of smoked salmon, the firm, slightly sweet dough is remarkably good.

Gefilte fish was another novelty, the recipe for which varies from household to household and from Mother to daughter. The fish in this Passover favourite can be served either boiled or fried, as fish balls or as a kind of fish cake. Passover is a time of remembrance, and for most families is a time to renew traditions and to celebrate the deliverance of the Israelites out of Egypt, under the guidance of Moses. I found I was fascinated by the actual Passover service held at table in each household, and deemed it a great privilege to be included, to learn the significance of the various special items on the table – the salt water, for example, which represents the tears of the Jewish people; the charoseth, which represents the clay used by the slaves in Egypt to make bricks (charoseth is made of apples, raisins, almonds and cinnamon); the horseradish, representing the bitterness, and the lamb shank bone for the Paschal lamb. The blood of the lamb marked the doors of the Jewish households to spare them from the plague that smote the Egyptians. Unleavened bread represents the bread that had no time to rise when the Israelites had to flee in great haste; a roasted egg is used as the Festival Offering.

As no leavened bread is eaten at this time, potato flour and matzo meal are used. My children loved them and we still to this day eat matzo biscuits with our cheese. I have many memories of visiting my girl friends on Fridays and watching spellbound as they prepared their different dishes! I remember the smell of the fish (which I must confess I didn't like too much) and the glorious warm cinnamon, spicy smell of the pastries and biscuits.

We grew to love many things from the Jewish kitchen. Strudels filled with fruit and nuts. Honeycake with red wine which is traditionally eaten at Easter. Blintzes, rolled pancakes filled with a mixture of curd cheese, egg, sugar and lemon, folded into a parcel and then deep-fried until golden and crispy. **Latkes**, potato cakes fried until crunchy and then dusted with icing sugar and cinnamon – you must eat them very hot. Hamantaschen, three-cornered pockets of sweet dough filled with a mixture often consisting of almonds, butter, honey, lemon juice, raisins and poppy seeds, vaguely reminscent of Danish pastries.

And, of course, cheesecakes. I didn't think I cared that much for them until I went to Leeds and tasted the variety to be found in every household, the recipes handed down, begged and copied. My favourite came from a special lady called Carol Bellow, who, with her husband Marshall took us in as house guests during the numerous brief visits we made from Bournemouth before we moved in and were frantically trying to keep tabs on the builders. Tired and fraught as we were after a long day stepping over planks, walking on joists and trying to get the electrician to give us a definite completion date, Carol would revive us with tea and a slice of her home-made **Cheesecake**. Years later I had the recipe from her and it is truly delicious.

Janet Williams is another good friend from those days: we produced our first-born within days of each other and pushed prams together thereafter. Her **Cheesecake** always graced the mums' tea at our offspring's birthday parties – a huge, fluffy, fruity creation.

I also became great friends with Lynn Greenwood who, after a spell in the Caribbean with her husband John, returned to England and settled in Yorkshire. With a now-flourishing furniture business, they live in a beautifully converted house in the picturesque hamlet of Kearby near Wetherby, and have settled down to coping with the English weather. They are guardians to our children – and when I had just produced my fourth, Lynn was heard to say, 'I do hope that's the lot!'

A keen gardener, Lynn has made a garden which is a tribute to her skill and patience. I gave her a fig tree one Christmas, six years ago, which flourished so well that two years later it burst out of the greenhouse and is yearly covered in delicious, juicy figs. In contrast, my poor effort, here in the Sunny South, struggles to produce six! Talking of fresh figs, have you tried them with Parma ham instead of melon? Cut them in half using a zig-zag cut, and then turn back the tips rather like a water-lily – attractive *and* delicious.

Lynn is a good cook who sticks to well-loved and familiar recipes. One of my favourites, almost more for its presentation than its taste, is her Beef Fillet en Croûte. A simple classic, but she spends hours shaping the pastry into a country cottage with doors, windows and chimney pots – all the details down to the roses at the door are there, almost too good to eat! Her **Spinach Roulade** is very easy to do and bound to impress, and her **Tomato Sauce** recipe is delicious, freezes well and is immeasurably useful for all sorts of dishes. I use it with Avocado Mousse and it is lovely with **Grandpa's Egg Mousse** for a change.

Jocelyn Frazier lived just across the lane from us. Her little daughter Lucy used to play with Sara, our first child, and we did a school run together. Tea at her house always included her **Lemon Cake** – light, rich and sweet/sharp with the lemon syrup on top. I can still see so clearly in my mind the coffee mornings we used to give – tables groaning under the assault of delicacies, the biscuits, quiches and rich chocolate cakes defied description.

Eating out in the North was another great source of pleasure, and we were very fortunate to have such a feast of good restaurants available to us, from the humble Mario and Franco's Pizza to the illustrious five-star Box Tree Cottage Restaurant at Ilkley. Favourite of all though, and the one we always return to on our visits to the North, is the Pool Court at Pool in Wharfedale, run by Michael Gill and his wife Hanni. A fine old Georgian house is the setting for the restaurant which was opened by the Gills in 1966, since when, thanks to their endless enthusiasm they have achieved the highest accolades. For me, however, the most attractive things are the cheerful welcome, the relaxed and friendly atmosphere and the sure knowledge that you are going to have an excellent evening in their company.

I remember the first time I ate **Scallops in Noilly Prat Sauce** at Pool Court. It was our wedding anniversary, and the weather was awful with thick snow and a hard frost. We slid all over the place driving to Pool but we were determined to get there, and the scallops – superb and very fresh – made it all worthwhile! Michael gave me the recipe and also that for **Calves' Liver in Citrus Sauce**, a particular favourite with Peter; I sometimes serve the liver with Framboise Sauce, which is equally good. The liver needs to be very thin so unless you have an exceptionally sharp knife and a good eye, ask your butcher to cut it wafer thin for you.

Casserole of Venison with Cherries is another of Michael's recipes – the marinated meat has a lovely flavour that is perfectly complemented by the cherries. When it comes to dessert time at Pool Court, I am always spoilt for choice. **Pears St Moritz** is very much a house speciality and one I often end up choosing. When you make it, try garnishing the plate with fresh sprigs of mint, a few raspberries and some tiny white flowers – and the compliments will come showering down!

I first tasted **Banoffi Pie** in a little restaurant called The Spice Box at Boston Spa. The restaurant was once a corner chemist's shop and had been cleverly converted. Small, and painted dark brown, it consisted of just two tiny rooms with a roaring fire in each. The walls were still lined with old rosewood boxes for storing herbs and medicines, their Latin names beautifully inscribed on them.

The menu was always simple and although you could criticize some of the dishes for being too saucy, everything was always well cooked, with hot plates, and beautifully presented. Pigeon Casserole, Beef en Daube, Pork Fillet with Prunes, Apple and Celery – they always served a dish of the day, sometimes rabbit, or game, often chicken done very much in the French manner with tarragon, or pot-roasted with olives, or the old favourite, Coq au Vin. There was almost a revolt when the owner/chef tried to take his Home-made Pâté off the menu and replace it with a more sophisticated one. Similar to my own recipe, it was creamy, smooth, a very uncomplicated liver pâté which was served with hot thick slices of crunchy white toast. **Tarragon Pears** was a starter I often had at the Spice Box, and before we left Yorkshire I requested the method.

Vegetables were simple, for instance jacket potatoes and a whole cauliflower covered in a perfect **Béchamel Sauce** popped in the centre of the table for all to help themselves (there was always something else available for non-cauli lovers!). Puds always posed a problem of choice. Fruit Cobblers, Banoffi Pie – consisting of toffee, cream and bananas – Mousses, Cheesecake made with hazelnut yoghurt, and delicious chocolatey, nutty, biscuity puds that I never managed to extract a recipe for.

Living in the North opened my eyes to the variety of different county and local dishes, and I became a fan of Elizabeth Ayrton. Several of her recipes have become favourites: **Huntingdon Stuffed Pears** is one, easy to make and delicious as a starter. In the 18th century the county of Huntingdon became famous for Stilton cheese, although in fact it originated from Leicestershire. Stilton was originally the only cheese made with double cream. Nowadays it is often factory-made with whole milk and no added cream, which makes for a more chalky texture. It is a marvellously versatile cheese and can be added to so many things.

Another of Elizabeth Ayrton's recipes that I often use is from 1870, an Oxford Savoury. Served in those days at the high table or sometimes at the Master's Lodge at Balliol College, it makes a change from puds and is a favourite with the men.

However, the most important acquisition from our Yorkshire days was not a recipe but a person! She was 'Annie' – Grannie T to everyone and beloved by us all. When we were desperate for a pair of capable, loving and experienced hands after I had produced my first-born and was trying to cope with a lifestyle that was getting busier by the day, I advertised for a locum Grannie – and along came Annie Turner. She has become Mum, Grannie and an intrinsic part of our lives. She has been a pillar of strength to me over the years and I can pay her no greater compliment than to say we all adore her. One of my children's favourites is **Grannie T's Flip** which she makes in tinfuls when she arrives (it's always gone within two days). She is a good simple Yorkshire cook and makes perfect Sponge Puds, Parkin, delicious Curd Tarts, tiny light Fairy Cakes, Yorkshire Puds that almost push their way out of the Aga – and she has my fridge organized within half an hour of being in the house. As one of my friends said, 'Everyone should have a Grannie T.'

She trained as a nurse at Pontefract Hospital in Yorkshire, went on the maternity ward with her 'babies', then had a spell at Clayton Hospital and eventually took a position at Pinderfields Hospital on Casualty. She and husband George produced a daughter, Hilary, and a son, John, and all went well until George sadly died in 1967. Not one to sit at home and grieve, she went back to nursing and carried on until 1973, then retired. That was when my guardian angel stepped in. She answered my advertisement and arrived in the Alliss household. Through mumps, chickenpox and whooping cough, she has been there, on hand, to cope. She kept me sane when my second daughter, Victoria, went into hospital at two months, and it was she who gave me the faith to have another child, Simon. When Henry was born the look of love and sheer pleasure on her face at the prospect of another baby to love and care for was magical. She is a truly special lady.

Blackmoor Farm was a homely and happy home for us. So many

good things happened there. I look back and think of the traditional Boxing Morning parties we gave when I was up all Christmas Night cooking for the 40 or 50 who would descend, starving for lunch on the 26th. One year my girl friend Pam was there, but not feeling too good, so I laughingly said, 'It's your age.' Three weeks later she burst into the kitchen and said, 'You and "It's your age" – I'm pregnant!' So we downed a bottle of wine to commiserate!

I remember Johnny Mathis sitting in our sunlit drawing room and confessing that he had played golf so badly that morning with my husband and his great friend Ronnie Sumrie that they had turned their heads away in embarrassment. Johnny had then sung 'Maria' at the top of his voice and laughingly shouted to the two stunned fellows, 'Thank God I can still sing!'

I remember taking a neighbour's child to school who proudly boasted, 'My Grandpa's got a new Rolls Royce,' and my son aged four retorted, 'So what. My Dad's just got a new toothbrush!' I remember too the agony of sitting in hospitals with little Victoria, of the ten months of living a quiet sort of hell learning to cope with the fact that she would never improve, let alone live for much longer. And I remember the sense of comfort that Peter and I discovered through being amongst friends.

CHAPTER FIVE

THE MOVE SOUTH

IN 1980, AFTER TEN VERY HAPPY YEARS in Yorkshire, we decided it was time to move back to the South of England. Peter was spending much more time in London, most of his work was in the South and I was beginning to get paranoiac about the long hours he spent driving up the M1 motorway, often in the early morning after a hard day's work or, worse, after a transatlantic flight. So, with many regrets, but with many warm and happy memories, we made our tearful farewells and one sunny morning in May 1980 we set off for Surrey.

We had already found a house, built at the turn of the century on a hill on the edge of the village of Churt. It was badly in need of renovation and just what I needed to 'get my teeth into'. We lodged with our friends David and Karen Wickins and set-to to cope – yet again – with the builders.

David was the Chairman of British Car Auctions, lately of Frimley and now at Blackbushe near Camberley, Surrey. A huge, handsome, ebullient man, generous to a fault and marvellous company, he and Peter met over 30 years ago and they have remained firm friends. Karen, his American wife, taught me to 'test' beef by putting a skewer right through the middle of the joint and, holding it there to count five. Draw it out and run your hand down it. For medium-rare beef it should be lukewarm in the centre and get progressively hotter towards the outside. It works every time.

Work went on at the house for five months until, after many

tears and pleas, and much cajoling, encouragement and frustration, we moved into Bucklands along with the brick dust. There were no carpets, half the floorboards were up and we had the added company of five builders; but with a bed to sleep in and my brand new Aga cooker, life was possible. Difficult, but possible. Grannie T arrived 'to help' and suddenly there was calm among the chaos.

Now, some seven years later, everything has come together and we all love our home. We built on a new kitchen wing to cope with our increasing family (another 12 months of agony – has anyone else tried to explain to a 14-month-old boy why he cannot hit the wall with a hammer like the builders do?). The garden is blossoming under Neil's experienced eye and the house runs smoothly with the help of Norma, our housekeeper. The children are all settled happily in schools within easy reach – Sara at the Royal Naval School, Haslemere, Simon at St Edmund's in Hindhead and Henry at the local St John's Primary School.

How well I remember first arriving at St John's School in Churt in 1980. School in the village for my five-year-old seemed to be a good way for him and me to make friends, so off we set one Monday morning in June. When I returned, some six hours later, to meet him coming out, a lady rushed up to me and said, all in one breath, 'Hello, I'm Pauline, I'd like to welcome you to Churt on behalf of the school governors.' I thought, 'Oh, hello, how do I get out of this?' That lady became one of my best friends and we often laugh about our 'suspect' start. She, like me, has two hungry school-age children and her quick **Corn Chowder** is great for Saturday lunch, served with crusty bread before they go out to brave the rugby field and frozen toes!

Simon stayed at that school for two very happy years before moving to St Ed's. It was quite an eye-opener for him to join a bigger school, where, for the first time, he realized Daddy was famous! After two weeks we were bombarded with questions such as 'Are we really very rich?' and 'Can I change my name from Alliss (Alice!)?' and 'Please, Dad, could I have your autograph 10 times as I have 10 friends willing to pay 10p a go!' This was acceptance in a big way! We had moved from the North partly because Peter, his partner David Thomas and Ken Wood, of 'Mixer' fame, were involved in the development of the Old Thorns Golf and Country Club, which was Ken's old country house set in rolling acres just outside Liphook in Hampshire. After a series of adventures and financial hiccoughs, the course was eventually sold in April 1984 to a Japanese company, London Kosaido, since when it has gone from strength to strength.

Gary Jones, the General Manager, and his very caring staff set a high standard and, along with suites of rooms, Japanese bath house, swimming pool, conference room and magnificently testing 18 holes of golf, they boast two superb restaurants, one European, cooking French classical and modern cuisine, and the other the only authentic Teppan-yaki restaurant south of London.

It is a sheer delight to eat Teppan-yaki (literally, 'iron grill'): ten or so courses of a quality hard to describe without waxing poetic. There are appetizers in the form of tiny rolls of smoked fish, marinated vegetables, and tiny spinach-wrapped cheesy parcels, all dipped into a delicious soya-based piquant sauce. Delicate soup, served in individual tiny china teapot-like containers, which you pour into fragile little bowls to drink. Fish next, the freshest salmon, scallops and calamars cooked in front of you on a sizzling hotplate presided over by a Japanese chef whose dexterity with a knife and palate knife is truly amazing. A smidgen of butter and oil is all that is needed, with fresh sea salt and garlic – the flavours are magnificent. Then comes salad, finely chopped cabbage and carrot, again in a piquant dressing, while slices of huge Spanish onion and green peppers are cooking. Everything, I hasten to add, is eaten with chopsticks! Rice is next on the menu, flicked up and around on the buttered hotplate with amazing ease; chunks of chicken are added and egg, and the rice finally emerges golden brown and delicious.

Savouring the rice, you can watch the meat course cooking. Fillet of beef in butter, tender and succulent with chopped mushrooms on the side. This is the point when you may think, 'Hmm, how much more?' Well, you're nearly there – just a bowl of golden crunchy beansprouts to follow and a chance to rest before the offer of delicately flavoured ice cream as a dessert. Sake (rice wine) is served throughout the meal and tiny cups of light Japanese green tea, instead of heavy coffee. The restaurant has three chefs and an assistant. Each is a specialist in a particular type of cooking, one for Teppan-yaki, one for Sushi (meaning rawfish and the one most people associate with Japan), and one for Washoku (meaning traditional, decorated Japanese food).

The European restaurant is run by Geoff Sutton. He trained at the Lythe Hill Hotel near Haslemere, and then moved on to the Manor Hotel at Midhurst before joining Old Thorns four years ago. Locally born and bred, he is happy in this home environment and has no desire to move on again. 'Why should I?' he said, 'I have everything here at Old Thorns and marvellous fresh local-grown produce thrown in!'

Peter and I were eating there some months ago with David and

Lyndsay Jacobs. 'Cook us something special,' demanded my husband and Geoff produced **Suprêmes of Chicken Langousté**. He was immediately hailed as 'King', they were so good. I asked for the recipe and have twice prepared them for dinner parties at home.

Yes, there are many good things to recommend in our new surroundings, not least (although sadly just retired) my marvellous French butcher, Paul Jeanroy, at Liphook. How I enjoyed my weekly visit to see Paul. Always I was greeted with a stream of rapid French: 'Bonjour ma petite. Comment vas-tu? Comment va Peter?' Small and round, an excitable and very French man, he was always guaranteed to burst into a gallic flood at anyone or anything! The shop itself was a veritable cornucopia of delicious terrines and pâtés, all freshly home-made, smoked hams, garlic sausages and every conceivable cut of meat. Ask Paul for advice or help and nothing was too much trouble. Fish, wet, glistening, very white, in a display that would not put Harrods to shame. Scallops, crabs, mussels, king prawns, lobsters, wild salmon – everything from humble coley to exotic turbot. Game of every description hanging in season, and anything you could not see, you only had to ask for.

Paul used to work as a youngster in his mother's hotel in Alsace-Lorraine. He told me Alsace was like a woman of the world. Both had passed through searing experiences with men of diverse nationalities, and had been governed by them in turn. They took on from all of them some intriguing characteristic to add to their own native beauty and had come through the assault enriched by the experience.

In Alsace-Lorraine, the polyglot atmosphere is reflected in their cuisine. Just think for a minute of the superb Pâté de Foie Gras Strasbourgeois, of Quiche Alsacienne – quite as excellent as its neighbour from Lorraine – and of the delicious dish of red beans that grow in practically every garden, Potée de Haricots Rouges. And who could forget the sweet Tarte aux Mirabelles (golden plums) or my favourite Tarte aux Quetsches, those beautiful perfumed sweet/sour purple plums. Alsatian wines are now recognized and loved by many – Ribeauvillé, Riquewihr, Molsheim and many others made from Riesling, Sylvaner and Traminer grapes.

Paul gave me a recipe for Poulet Sauté Riesling a l'Alsacienne. Simply roast a chicken in a mirepoix of vegetables; when cooked, quarter it, put into a serving dish and keep warm, and then cover with a sauce made of lightly fried mushrooms, the mirepoix of vegetables thickened with a Beurre Manié and a good glassful of Riesling. Add half a cup of Worcestershire Sauce and finish with some cream and parsley. Eat it with sauté potatoes, followed by salad.

My husband first met Paul at the Coq d'Or Restaurant in London, during the 1953 Ryder Cup matches. The team was taken out for dinner by Mr Lou Freedman, a golf supporter who was marvellously generous to the game; he thought 'the boys' deserved a good night out. And good it was; my husband never forgot the experience and it was a great joy for us to 'find' Paul again, 17 years later, in Hampshire. So many favourites have come from Paul with his inborn sense of economy and natural gift for invention. He always used to say that flavouring should enhance and suggest, not change. The shop is now under the excellent and watchful eye of Mr Read, a gentleman who is upholding its traditions and quality – but I do miss my exuberant Frenchman.

Paul's **Potage Lorrain** is a dish I often make during the winter months. Thick and filling, it is one of the children's favourites for an early supper after school. Moules in season, fresh and shiny and simply cooked with lots of fresh parsley and hunks of farmhouse bread to dunk in the juice. Eat them, as Paul does, for lunch, followed by a ripe Camembert, celery, grapes and, naturally, a bottle of very chilled dry white wine! His recipe for **Fillets of Sole à la Chantal** is another favourite. I rushed into his shop one day, panic-stricken, as my dearly beloved had arrived home with four for lunch and I had nothing but some cheese in the house. 'Pas de problème, ma petite,' smiled Paul, and ten minutes later I was home again clutching 12 fillets of sole which, following Paul's instructions, took 10 minutes to prepare and 25 to cook. Lunch was a huge success and the recipe went into the book!

Pheasant is not everyone's choice – we love it but prefer it casseroled to roasted because the meat stays much more moist. Talking to Paul one day, he gabbled out his own method (**Pheasant à la Jeanroy**). 'Stop,' I shouted, whipped out a pen and wrote down what he said. Even guests who normally don't care for game eat it this way – and ask for a second helping!

Surrey is blessed with many excellent eating places, and the Frensham Ponds Hotel, on the road from Farnham to Hindhead, is just one of the many. Until recently run by Michael Katzler, Head Chef Andrew Stanford and his excellent staff, the hotel is a mature, white-rendered building sitting peacefully overlooking Frensham Big Pond with its yacht club, and wind-surfers gliding across the lake.

The origins of the building are something of a mystery. It may have been a monastery under the jurisdiction of Waverley Abbey, then around 1800 it became a farmhouse, then an inn, The White Horse, noted for being a gambling haunt for the young blades from Farnham and Army officers from Aldershot. Finally, around 1900, it became a hotel under the guidance of a Mr Griffiths and has progressed from there to the first-class hotel complex it is today.

It is generally believed that there was a Roman farm to the north of the pond and that the pond itself was a small basin fed by a natural spring. Some time before 1208 a dam was built to make the pond the size it is today. Stocked with fish, it was part of the manorial estate belonging to the Bishop of Winchester; this is noted in the Winchester Pipe Rolls which contain the yearly accounts of the Sheriff of the county. The fish were supplied to the Bishops of Guildford and Farnham Castle, and accounts, we learn, had to be rendered to the Winchester Pipe Rolls from all the fisheries and farms in the area. Nowadays, there is no fishing and the area has been declared a nature park. The council, in its wisdom, and with quite a lot of local protest, have put in car parks and cordoned off other areas for replanting and reseeding, a necessary operation in view of the tourists attracted there during the summer. Another point of local interest – and I wish I'd been around to see it – occurred in 1913 when the first seaplane to fly was brought from Farnborough to Frensham Pond. There, much to the amazement of the locals, it successfully took off and landed. I would have loved to have seen some of their faces!

We often dine at the Frensham Ponds and it is a favourite for Sunday lunch. We eat in the tranquillity of the long dining room with its wide windows overlooking the water and the colourful sails of the yachts, then have coffee and Michael's delicious **Engadina** while the children work off their lunch and high spirits feeding the ducks on the landing stage beneath.

I've never been a great fan of fish soups and for a long time the only place that I had enjoyed them was in France and, in particular, on the Brittany coast near La Baule. Then we found the Links at Liphook, which is known locally as the 'Crab and Lobster' from the abundance of fresh fish and shellfish it serves daily. Richard and Esther Grace have been in charge since 1978 and the dining room is cosy with warm lighting, the ceiling hung with fishing nets and lobster pots – and Esther's fish soup is perfection. It is always a must for me when it's on the menu. 'It *must* be made with stock from fish shells – no stock cubes,' says Esther. Part of the fun of the evening is talking to Sergio – the Maître d' Sergio Bertolo, who has been in England for 17 years now and is still as Italian as he was when he first set foot on these shores! One catches three words out of 100, which makes conversation difficult, but

Sergio's beaming face makes up for everything!

They also serve the best crab sandwiches that I have ever tasted. Peter and I dropped in at lunchtime some two years ago and, several sandwiches and glasses of chilled House White later, we found ourselves on the way home clutching two tiny rabbits, presents from Esther for the children! They were a lasting souvenir of our day. The two tiny babies were half wild and we spent the rest of the summer chasing them round the garden as they constantly ate their way out of every cage we put them into. Eventually they made good their escape but obviously decided they liked the area – so they multiplied in great numbers, much to the children's delight and my husband's horror!

When we arrived in Surrey, I left behind me in Yorkshire my hairdresser, Janet. After 10 years spent together coping with my hair, we knew each other well and, as all ladies know, hairdressers are very personal people; rather like our doctors, we hate changing them. Then we moved and, after two months of builders, my hair badly needed attention; the brick dust, paint and traumas were taking their toll.

I set off for the local town to find a salon, and came across Jon's, in Haslemere. After requesting a shampoo and set, in due course I was escorted to the basins to be met by Rod, the owner and senior stylist who, upon seeing me, took one bedraggled lock of hair between thumb and finger, grimaced and said, 'Whoever has been doing your hair?' I was so mad at the seeming lack of loyalty between hairdressers, I spluttered, 'Please, say no more. Wash it, set it and I shall not trouble you again!'

I seethed quietly under the hands of the shampooist and, just as I was about to move to the next chair, the wind was totally taken out of my sails by Rod dropping to his knees in front of me, head in hands, and, with a wicked twinkle, saying, 'Please, can we start all over again?' I burst into laughter and from that dubious start we have become very good friends.

Rod works a long day, with not much chance to eat, so his wife Joan sends him in with chunks of her **Farmhouse Loaf Cake** – just to keep him going. While I was sitting under the dryer one morning, my tummy was rumbling so hard he took pity on me and passed over a slice. It was so good, I immediately begged the recipe from Joan. She did say, by the way, that it must be made with 6 oz (175 g) Blue Band and butter mixed; it's definitely not so good with either all one or the other.

Now Peter and I were back in the South, we were able to revisit all our old friends and haunts. The Dormy Hotel at Ferndown is one of them and very much part of the Alliss story. Peter was born in Berlin when Percy, his father, was the Professional at Wannsee Golf Club. But, with the rumblings of Hitler and the Nazis growing louder, in 1931 Percy decided it was time to move his family back to England. There has always been a 'family story' of Mother Alliss stuffing banknotes into her undergarments to get them out of Germany, an episode which led to the family saying, 'Mother said knickers to Hitler!'

After a short spell at Beaconsfield Golf Club, Bucks, and another short spell at the Temple Newsam Golf Club in Yorkshire, the Allisses moved south in 1938 to Ferndown, Dorset, where Percy was offered the position of Professional at Ferndown Golf Club. They found a house opposite the course and stayed there for the rest of their days. The Dormy Hotel was just across the road and made a marvellous watering hole for Percy. A few years ago they opened a Sportsman's Bar with an Alliss Corner featuring many old mementos and Ryder Cup photographs of Alliss Senior and Junior.

When Percy frequented the Dormy it was a small hotel, grown out of three private houses that were, in time, converted into a nursing home and then into a hotel. In the 1960s the hotel was added to the De Vere Group, and now under the Greenall Whitney umbrella it has a superb leisure club, 140 bedrooms, conference facilities and a wonderful restaurant. I stayed there in the late summer of 1986 with Grannie T and the children and begged the **Pork Stew with Sauerkraut** recipe, not because it reminded me of Germany but because the Head Chef assured me it was one of the early recipes that my father-in-law had loved. I'm not at all sure of the authenticity of that remark (!) but the recipe itself, for sauerkraut lovers, is well worth trying.

CHAPTER SIX

TRAVELS IN THE UK

PETER RETIRED FROM international golf in 1970. He had started commentating for the BBC during his playing years, but now, slowly, with more time, he became further involved working closely with Henry Longhurst, the king of golf writers and a master commentator.

HENRY LONGHURST

Henry was a fascinating man and his friendship with my husband was to progress from comradeship to an almost father-son relationship as the years rolled by. Both respected and loved each other and Peter, in a small way, helped to fill the gap in Henry's life caused by losing both his son and son-in-law in tragic circumstances.

Henry, I discovered, was a man of huge talents and literary skills, vastly experienced in so many fields from the microphone to the House of Commons. I loved hearing his tales of his early life and how, originally from Bedford, his family had owned a store in the town called Longhurst & Skinner. He went up to Cambridge, won a Blue at golf, and became an active member of the Cambridge Golfing Society. This, in turn, introduced him to some of the famous names of the day, some of whom became life-long friends. There was Lord Castleross, the diarist of the Thirties; Lord Brabazon, a lover of golf and aviation, whose FLY 1 car registration plate was well known in motoring circles; and

Brigadier-General Critchley, the man who introduced this country to greyhound racing!

Henry married his half-French wife, Claudine at the onset of World War II. They were twice bombed, losing everything they had, and this later caused Henry to say, 'It rid us of the obsession for belongings!' Certainly, when we knew him he travelled light – one small suitcase with a few personal bits and pieces including a well-worn, well-thumbed edition of *The Wind in the Willows* which gave him enormous pleasure and comfort when he was low in spirits or tired.

In 1943 Henry was asked to stand as the Conservative Candidate for Acton during Churchill's time as leader. Although he won his seat, his political days were short-lived as he was ousted at the 1945 General Election. This led him back to doing what he loved, and did best, golf and writing. During his long years of writing for the *Sunday Times*, it was said by many of his fans that he not only contributed to the sales of the paper, he kept it going!

When I met Henry he was sadly already not in the best of health, but his sense of humour and his eye for a well-turned ankle kept me very amused. I remember sitting with him in amiable silence in a hospitality room at Gleneagles Hotel. Henry's head was down, he was clasping a pink gin to his midriff, and he appeared not to see the young lady in front of us wearing the tightest pair of trousers I had ever seen and no evidence of anything underneath. Bending over, she presented an excellent target and suddenly a voice grumbled beside me, 'Oh, I wish I had a peashooter with me!!' I learnt never to underestimate Henry!

He became godfather to our middle son, Simon, an honour our golf-playing 12 year-old is quietly very proud of. One of his prized possessions is his Christening tankard inscribed 'S.P.G.A. from H.L.'

The Longhursts lived for many years in two converted windmills – Jack and Jill – on the hill above the village of Hassocks, a few miles north of Brighton. They built a single-storey house between the two mills in which they lived, and Jill was made into a huge, book-lined, circular study for Henry. The first time I visited them was in 1972, when Peter and Henry were going to film the BBC Christmas golf review at The Windmills. It was an inclement day, damp and cold with a howling wind, and I remember Peter saying quietly to me, 'Don't, for heaven's sake, say to Henry how windy it is.' I gathered many visitors did so and Henry's inevitable response was a growling, 'Yes! That's why they built windmills up here!' Safe inside, however, with Claudine's smiling welcome, I felt immediately warm and at home.

Lunch for the 'team' started with the most delicious **Carrot**

Soup, served thick, piping hot and in large French soup bowls with crusty bread. We ate at a long oak table – dozens of us, it seemed. There was the BBC, us, masses of Henry's friends, the grandchildren – all talking and laughing at once. It was a memorable day, and Claudine's soup has become a much-loved recipe in our household.

Henry was also responsible for my love of game. My own parents were not keen, so as a child I really never appreciated the finer points of grouse. But at Gleneagles one year Henry insisted that I should 'never turn down the offer of grouse and most excellent claret on the Glorious Twelth!' That changed everything. Since the schedule for filming the Pro-Celebrity Golf programme always coincided with that date, it became a well-established yearly ritual and, to this day, we raise our glasses to absent friends on 12 August.

During the filming of the Pro-Celebrity matches Claudine and I used to do our own thing. I sometimes followed a few holes of a match; occasionally I went antique hunting in local villages, or visited one of the numerous woollen mills in the area.

Claudine used to collect her basket, her water-colours and sketch pad and settled down under Henry's commentary box. Once there she would sketch the views, collect and press any wild flowers within reach and generally absorb the countryside. Somehow it hardly ever rained. Those days were good for me, too, because I am by nature a restless soul and Claudine taught me to sit, relax and absorb the surrounding beauty. 'And all for free,' she used to say.

GLENEAGLES, TURNBERRY AND NAIRN

The Pro-Celebrity series stayed at Gleneagles for several consecutive years and we loved it. The grandeur of the place – the breathtaking scenery that faced you whichever window you looked out of. The crisp, sunny autumn days when the very grass sparkled in the late sunshine and the hills surrounding the four courses seemed forever changing colour from clear blues to deep mauves; the yellow gorse, the heathers and the spectacular view up the Glen of the Eagles through the Ochils. The walk through the grounds to the course led down stone, lichen-lined steps, then a winding path took you to the wooden bridge across the stream and so to the clubhouse and the professional's shop; there the lilting voice of Ian Marchbank welcomed us 'once more' to Gleneagles. Big John McIvarry, hall porter *extraordinaire*, always waiting to greet us at the impressive front door of the hotel, remembering every child, every name and every guest, and Billy, his Irish 'first lieutenant', who could organize 'the impossible'. Happy days!

And, of course, there were the celebrities themselves. One I recall was the wife of a well-known American actor. This lady usually carried on as though she was ever-so-slightly superior but, when we got caught in the rain on a shopping trip to Perth, pulled out a Gleneagles Hotel shower cap and placed it firmly on her head. It's difficult to be superior in a plastic bath hat!

The barriers of etiquette were almost breached on another occasion when James Hunt tried to walk shoeless and tieless into the dining room for dinner one night, followed by Oscar, his huge Alsatian! Great, too, was my embarrassment when I 'lost' my two year-old son and found he had pushed his way into James's room and, wearing nothing but his nappy, was carrying on an earnest conversation with James who was in the bath at the time. Red-faced, I hauled my son out!

Meeting my personal heroes was a special thrill. At Gleneagles I not only said hello to the unforgettable Bing Crosby, I actually walked up the fairway chatting to him! And Howard Keel. Who can ever forget *Seven Brides for Seven Brothers?* Years later he made a return appearance at Turnberry and my daughter, aged 12, was dumbstruck because, as Miss Ellie's husband in *Dallas*, he was a hero to her too! And there he was, singing for one of those unforgettable impromptu concerts in the early hours when all inhibitions were gone, with Bruce Forsyth on the piano, Kenny Lynch and Denis Morgan (of *Rose-Marie* fame!) on vocals and some half-dozen of us joining in the chorus – not to mention the dancing.

Then in the early 1980s Gleneagles was sold and, for political and business reasons, the series moved back to Turnberry on the Ayrshire coast – and a spectacularly different venue. The hotel, under the watchful eye of General Manager Chris Rouse, has become a firm favourite of ours. Perhaps it has something to do with the ever-changing mood of the weather, or the glorious fresh tangy sea winds that blow every remnant of city dust out of one's eyes and hair and cause such chaos to the golfers on the Ailsa and Arran courses. The sudden change to glorious warm, balmy days when the sea shimmers and Ailsa Rock stands proud and imperious in her isolation, some 10 miles out to sea.

The hotel was built at the turn of the century, the result of the golf-mad Marquis of Ailsa building a private golf course on his Culzean estate. This course was, in turn, taken over by the Glasgow and South Western Railway, forging a link with the railway that was to last over 70 years. With broadening communications and a new railway station it soon became evident that a hotel was needed to complete the link, and by 1906 the hotel, the golf course and the railway began to flourish. But with the dark clouds of war threatening, the hotel was taken over as a training station for pilots of the Royal Flying Corps and Commonwealth flying units. To this day, a memorial can be seen on the hill above the present 12th hole. Once it was relinquished by the War Office, Ailsa became the venue for the British Ladies' Open Championship and in the late 1920s the course was redesigned; but before much could be made of the new shape, Hitler's war arrived, and much of the new work was undone by the new tenants, RAF Coastal Command. Instead of pitchmarks, tees and greens, Turnberry became again an airbase with hangars, airsocks and runways.

It was 1949 before work began to restore Ailsa to her former glory and it was 1951 before the mammoth task was completed. Today, the coastal stretch of holes, turbulent dunes and rocky crags, with the lighthouse jutting out into the sea, symbolizes golf at its best and, with two British Open Golf Championships in her crown, Ailsa's future seems brightly secure.

The dining room at the Turnberry Hotel is large, airy and spacious with long sweeping windows overlooking the golf course, the sea and Ailsa Craig. Dining in the soft evening glow of the magnificent sunsets is an indescribable pleasure, all this under the watchful eye of Luigi, the Maître d', whilst behind the scenes calm reigns supervised by Master Chef Duncan Stewart Cameron. A marvellously down-to-earth Scot with deep farming roots, he describes his food as traditional, using good raw materials, and would admit also to being greatly influenced by the new cooking techniques of Nouvelle and Minceur, though only to the extent of lightening his food. Classically trained, starting at the Lochalsh Hotel, he moved on to the Caledonian Hotel in Edinburgh and from there, after five years, to the London Ritz. Still wanting to spread his wings, he joined the Elbow Beach Surf Club in Bermuda where he developed his interest in fish (and had 40 different varieties to play with). Summoned back to his beloved Scotland and Gleneagles, he married his wife, Joy, and today is at the top of his profession at Turnberry Hotel.

I spent two very happy hours in the hotel kitchen, listening and watching during the run-up to dinner. I recommend you to try Duncan's **Langoustine au Gingembre**, easy to make and indeed very special. His **Earl Grey Parfait** is a particular favourite of mine and typical of Duncan Cameron's desire for simple, unusual food.

Have you ever thought that golfers are about the only sportsmen who do not break off play for bad weather unless the course is actually flooded or there is lightning about? There they are, come rain or shine, plodding their way up the fairways towards the clubhouse where a hot toddy awaits them in wintry weather or a cooling glass of something else when it's fine – and food.

Perhaps that is why meals are so important to golfers. They need food which is filling, sustaining, and not too heavy on the tum, and in recognition of these needs most clubhouses nowadays boast a high standard of catering. Having watched my husband playing up the Turnberry links soaked to the skin, I have wondered whether Cock-a-leekie Soup was maybe invented for golfers!

While talking of Scotland, I must mention another golfer's hotel that is a particular favourite of ours, the Golf View Hotel in Nairn. Sitting on the sheltered shore of the Moray Firth, overlooking the mysterious Black Isle, its almost austere exterior makes a big contrast with the warmth of welcome that guests receive from General Manager Greta Anderson, also with the unsurpassed excellence of the meals prepared by Head Chef Willie McCloud.

The old guest book from 1897 shows that the hotel was built originally as a 10-bed hotel by a Mr James Ellis, but with bits added in 1914 and again in 1931 it has become a 55-bed hotel whose guests tend to be families and friends who return year after year for the comfort, peace and tranquillity, and the friendliness of the staff. The flyleaf of the original guest book has this inscription:

> 'Long may thy halls, the jaded travelor rest
> And grateful memories haunt the parting guest
> May eager longing lead him to repeat
> His frequent visits to this quiet retreat.'
> *April 1897*

Somehow I feel Mr James Ellis would have been very proud.

I loved the food at this hotel and begged the recipe for **Cullen Skink Soup**. One memorable night in April 1986, when Peter and I were staying as guests for a dinner given by the Highlands and Islands Tourist Board to promote golfing holidays in the Scottish Highlands, the menu consisted of the following. A Roulade of Smoked Salmon filled with the lightest prawn and tomato mousse and served with a delicate Pernod dressing. A Game Consommé followed, flavoured with juniper berries, piping hot and topped with a light, flaky pastry lid. Medallions of Angus Beef Fillet, baked with a most unusual Chicken and Goat's

Cheese Soufflé and served on a sauce made from a reduction of port, pickled walnuts and rich meat glaze. This was served with a marvellous selection of fresh, lightly cooked vegetables.

The dessert was a triumph, and one I have adapted and copied since: a brandy snap basket dipped in half white and half dark chocolate and filled with a mouth-watering fresh strawberry cream and garnished with kiwi fruit. It was so good I could hardly wait to get home and have a go at it myself. A selection of Scottish cheeses and oatcakes was followed by coffee with Greta's home-made Tablet, a sort of rich home-made fudge. I could quite see why guests return to this hotel year after year.

TREVOSE

Tournament golf and television have meant travelling all over the British Isles and Peter and I have many favourite stopping places; Trevose, in North Cornwall, close to the fishing town of Padstow, would have to be near the top of the list. Trevose was the scene of an 'Around with Alliss' in 1986. The course and holiday chalets are owned by an old friend, Peter Gammon, and his wife Caroline. Small, slightly rounded, with a mischievous twinkle in his eye, Peter runs the complex with a firm hand – and has been known to shout at people for slow play!

My Peter has, for many years, regarded Trevose and Peter G. as his personal bolthole, the ideal place for a leisurely daily round of 18 holes and an even more leisurely drink at the bar – and I can actually see the stress falling off him! At the heart of things is a comfortable rambling house, built close to the sea and sand dunes and overlooking Trevose Head. The Gammons run a busy household, full of people, kids, barking dogs – a bit like a home from home!

One of my best memories is of the evening Peter G. threw a dinner party. He produced two bottles of Château Lafite '61 just before dinner, and we two wives overheard him whisper to my husband, 'This decanter is ours – the other decanter, of slightly inferior brew, is for them.' The two of them chuckled quietly like naughty schoolboys and then praised the wine, its colour and bouquet all through the meal, raising their glasses in silent glee to one another.

For an informal supper one night we had Caroline's **Fillet of Pork Normandy**, and I begged the recipe. Her **Chilled Lemon Flan** is a must for anyone with children; mine adore it and so do all the

Gammons' friends. It is quick to make and if you do two at a time the second, without the cream topping, freezes beautifully.

FOLLOWING THE OPEN

Many of our annual travels are connected with the championship that is generally thought of as the world's major golf event: the British Open. Played traditionally on a links course within sight and sound of the sea, the venue moves between St Andrews in Scotland, the home of golf and the most famous course of all, Muirfield, Royal Lytham, Royal Birkdale, Royal St George's (the only southern venue), Royal Troon and Turnberry. My favourites would have to be St Andrews and Muirfield, not so much from a golfing point of view, but because they hold so many happy memories.

Captain Jack Anderson – Jock to his friends – and Elsie, his wife, have been our hosts on many occasions. They live at Dairsie, some seven or eight miles west of St Andrews. Their home is a stern but magnificent, white rendered and fortified Scottish house made softer by rolling lawns, strutting peacocks and gardens that, under Elsie's watchful eye and green fingers, would do credit to Kew Gardens. I so clearly remember my first visit. I had heard such a lot about these marvellous friends from my husband, but nothing prepared me for the reality.

Jock is a lawyer by profession, a member of the Royal and Ancient Golf Club, a quarry owner, soft-fruit farmer and a past President of the Royal Caledonian Curling Society. Heavens! I thought, a formidable man!

He stood in the doorway, on that first visit, a tall man in tartan trews, an open-necked shirt and an old comfortable-looking sports jacket, complete with red hanky flowing from the breast pocket. As he beamed a welcome, I suddenly felt as if I'd known this kindly man all my life – indeed, as the days went by, I came to see how much, in many ways, he reminded me of my own father.

Elsie, his wife, is a lovely and remarkable lady. Small, auburn-haired and wiry, unashamedly a chain-smoker and possibly the only person left in the world who is still able to find, buy and smoke full-strength, unfiltered Golf Flake cigarettes, her frail countenance belies her enormous inner strength and enthusiasm for coping with life, with Jock and with her other great love, her garden. Scottish hospitality, for me, took a new turn when I was confronted with the abundance of fare on her table, from the tureens of piping hot, creamy porridge which greeted us at breakfast, to the candle-lit dining table and succulent joints of Angus beef, followed by Scottish cheeses and all helped sweetly down by carefully selected wines from Jock's considerable cellar. And at every meal during the fruit season, bowlfuls of sweet strawberries and perfect raspberries picked that day from their own fields.

CHAMPAGNE!

How could one leave the Open Championship and the BBC without mentioning Anthony Leschallus and Bollinger Champagne? A mad-keen golfer, Anthony decided that the Open Championship was a natural venue for promoting champagne and in 1969, at Royal Lytham St Annes – the year in which we had a British winner in Tony Jacklin – the first Bollinger tent appeared. It was indeed a year to remember! A champagne tent was an innovation and was viewed with not a little scepticism by many. 'Too expensive – never catch on,' was the cautious comment, but from a humble beginning when, in that first year, only 100 bottles were used, and on Anthony's admission most of those were given away, the Bollinger tent has gone from strength to strength. During the 1986 Championship, 1,500 bottles were sold from the now-familiar, red and white striped tent and it has established itself as *the* meeting place. Rather like 'See you under the clock at Waterloo Station,' the cry has become 'See you at noon in the Bolly tent.'

There tales are swapped, acquaintances renewed, old friendships revived, famous faces seen, while the Press hover, scenting out the stories. The atmosphere sparkles, as do the glasses of bubbling champagne in everyone's hand.

Under the strong helm of Chairman Anthony Leschallus, and his co-directors – son Simon, Adrian Laird-Craig, Nicholas Strachan, Neville Archer and Sir John Baddley, not to forget Nicholas Liddle, without whom no selling team would be complete – the marquee is staffed by a team of pretty girls and a couple of strong fellows, led by Anthony's daughters, Marie-Louise and Joanna, and second son William. Anthony joined Menzendorf in 1958 when it was still a partnership in St James's, then in 1959–60 Menzendorf was bought by Bollinger and Anthony remained, rising to Chairman and Managing Director in 1972. A very good friend of ours, he is a big man, soft-spoken, with a quick sense of humour and blessed with a super wife, Lindy, and a close-knit family life. His roots are strong in the wine business, the family Leschallus deriving, they think, from the Huguenots who arrived on these shores in the late 17th century, their branch probably coming from the Provence area of France. The name Leschallus fascinated me and I asked what it meant. Translated it means vine pole (*échalas*) and their crest is just that – a vine growing up a pole.

Great Britain has long been an important market for champagne, and since the reign of Queen Victoria the House of Bollinger has held an Appointment as Purveyors of Champagne to the Royal Household. Today, the Bollinger vineyards are identified with a family devoted to creating and sustaining careful expansion with a strong emphasis on quality. Listening to Anthony talking about the 'House', the room grows quiet as he recounts the story of Madame Bollinger, known as 'La Grande Dame du Champagne', who, after the death of her husband in 1941, took over the firm's management in one of the most difficult periods in its history, and was responsible for its initital expansion. She was, indeed still is, obviously much loved and respected by her staff.

They still follow the most proven methods for quality. Thus, for wines with long ageing cycles, such as Grand' Année, Brut, Vintage and Bollinger de Bollinger R.D., the traditional fermenting in oak casks is used during the period of cellar ageing. I make no excuses for quoting Mme Bollinger, when in 1961 she said these immortal words:

> 'I drink champagne when I'm happy and when I'm sad.
> Sometimes I drink it when I'm alone.
> When I have company I consider it obligatory,
> I trifle with it when I'm not hungry and drink it when I am.
> Otherwise I never touch it unless I'm thirsty.'

What a remarkable lady!

And what a remarkable produce. Put it into soups; try champagne and Camembert; it's fantastic with fish, lending a subtle flavour all its own. Try drinking pink champagne with tiny wild strawberries floating on the top for a very special summer celebration. I was with Peter in Alicante, Spain the first time I drank pink champagne. Ajax were playing Real Madrid in a big football match, and I, against all popular opinion, backed the Dutch team, Ajax, to win. We won, and my prize was pink champagne with masses of those tiny sweet-sharp wild strawberries floating on the top. It was unforgettably good!

I also love Champagne Sorbet, with a delicate flavour that is almost unsurpassed. I watched, fascinated, in the Turnberry kitchens last year, as Head Chef Duncan Cameron gave me a lesson on making sorbets. It's so easy with the right equipment, and there is an almost endless variety of flavours to be had using all the mouth-watering types of fruit available in the shops. Everything from paw-paws and mangoes to the delicious tiny sweet clementines that arrive in the shops just in time for the Christmas festivities.

And who could overlook that famous drink, Bucks Fizz. A pick-me-up for jaded spirits, a reviver for jaded heads and sheer delight at any time. Bucks Fizz was introduced in 1921, at Bucks Club, London, by the resident barman, Malachy McGarry. It is made with two parts champagne and one part freshly squeezed orange juice, served very cold in tulip glasses – nothing could be nicer at 12 noon on a Sunday morning. Or at any time, come to think of it!

All the good things in life are associated with 'bubbly': births, weddings, Christenings, 21sts, anniversaries and, indeed, all the big social and sporting events. In my own opinion, no-one organizes such things better than we, the British. Think of warm, sunny Wimbledons; tea on the lawn and bowls of strawberries and cream. Ascot, with its magical yearly fashion show, the ladies wandering around in feathers, silk and big-brimmed hats, clutching their glasses of bubbly and pretending that their high heels are not really sinking into the grass beneath them! And the men, elegant and debonair in their morning dress and, I'm sure, half of them only doing it to please their wives!

And my personal favourite, Royal Henley Regatta, to which we often go in the company of David and Karen Wickins. Sitting in the sunshine on the terrace of Phylis Court overlooking the river, sipping Bollinger and watching the rowers racing towards the finishing point beneath us. We are lucky now to live in this very privileged world; it is not one to take too much for granted, but is certainly a world to enjoy, while it lasts.

CHAPTER SEVEN

ENTERTAINING OUR FRIENDS

GOLF HAS BEEN VERY KIND to us over the years. It is a fascinating sport to be involved in, one that commands respect from everyone, and is played on some of the loveliest stretches of land one can find in God's clear open fresh air, both at home and abroad.

When we moved down South we came back within visiting reach of Cliff and Jean Michelmore, friends of long standing. Indeed Cliff is godfather to our middle son, Simon. They live in a delightful rambling old town house in Reigate, full of old-world charm and antiques. Jean's lovely touches are to be seen in every room. She is a super cook, and the kitchen is the hub of the household for father, son Guy and daughter Jennie, and many's the happy evening we've had sitting round the scrubbed pine table, reminiscing and savouring the memory of a marvellous meal and the anticipation of the port to come! Jean's announcement that we were to have **Sussex Pond Pudding** gave us a lot of laughs but when it was cooked and turned out and the middle dropped into the 'pond' of delicious lemony goo, the laughs turned to rapt admiration!

Entertaining has always been one of our great pleasures. I can think of nothing nicer than to have friends and acquaintances around our dining table, with maybe the stimulus of new faces and new topics of conversation and the added prospect of making new friendships.

OUR BANQUET

The highlight, I suppose, of our entertaining came in November 1985 when we held a 'Grand Banquet' with Alan and Judy Payne (of Payne & Gunter, the caterers). The idea for a banquet came one day in the late summer when Alan, visiting us, caught my husband engaged in deep conversation on the 'phone and was instructed to fetch 'a bottle'.

Some ten minutes later we found him inspecting our 'cellar', and several bottles of Château Lafite '61 in particular. 'They should be drunk,' he enthused, 'in style, with the right people and food to complement.' So, with the help of Tom O'Shea, the company's Head Chef, we planned our banquet.

Alan Payne is the son of the late Gus Payne, a legendary figure of Dickensian appearance who was well known at all the principal catering and sporting venues. Small, rotund and bewhiskered, he always wore a fresh flower in his buttonhole, a Norfolk jacket, a waistcoat with a full 'hunter' and immaculately polished shoes that he changed at least four times a day. Gus was truly a character! He was born in Shepherds Bush in 1911, and his mother had a small coffee stall in Wandsworth. From such small beginnings grew the Payne catering organization.

Alan followed a little less flamboyantly in father's footsteps. He was leased out to other firms as part of his education in catering. Payne's went into golf in the mid-Fifties and in 1986 celebrated their 200th golf tournament with the Benson & Hedges at York. Of course, hospitality catering is now a huge business but it was at the Wentworth Club, Virginia Water, in the mid-Sixties that it really took off. If you look now at the vast showbiz arena at every championship event, with the rows of tents, exhibitions, banks, hotdog and sweet stalls (not to mention the official tents of the Championship Committee, you realize how big it has become and how large a part the caterers play.

Alan has a lovely, quick sense of humour, and I well remember one casual conversation with him about Payne and Gunter and how Payne joined forces with Gunter. In the 1820s James Gunter was an aristocratic subaltern in the Dragoons, and was credited with saying superciliously to a fellow officer one day, 'I understand, Sir, that your father is a confectioner. I wonder that you are not one also.' To which the other replied, 'And I understand, Sir, that your father was a gentleman...' From Alan, I also heard the story of how the Sirloin of

Beef came to be called. Much favoured as a joint by King Henry VII, he decided to knight it, so that henceforth it would be called not just the humble 'loin' but 'Sirloin'!

But enough of these digressions – we had a banquet to plan. It was the bicentenary year of Payne & Gunter, so Alan suggested we use one of their commemorative menus, and thought the one for Edward VII would be most suitable. Agreed. Then we turned our thoughts to our guests and the table. It was decided that we, the Allisses, should 'host' the night, take care of the wines and prepare the table, while Alan would provide the chef, the staff and the food. And what fun it turned out to be!

I spent the day of the party laying the table and doing the flowers. For the centrepiece I chose a long low arrangement, using silvery greens and palest pink to complement the pale green candles in the old silver candlesticks. It looked marvellous. Gleaming silver cutlery competed with the heavy Waterford crystal, while proudly flanking the top and bottom of the centrepiece were two firm, perfect pineapples on their silver bases. These, with the addition of the original Payne's palest green silk napkins, were Alan's finishing touches. Pineapples, he explained, became the symbol of hospitality after they were first grown by James II's gardeners at Darnlea Court, near Windsor. The fashion was taken up and spread from table to special ornamental work; pine-apple designs were carved on door frames, door knobs, gateposts, newel posts, even door knockers.

What bliss it was to watch the hustle and bustle of the Payne's vans arriving, to see my kitchen stripped and cleared for action, and then to be able to leave it all in Tom's capable hands and return for a long leisurely perfumed bath.

We decided 12 was a good number for our Banquet. They would consist of ourselves (Allisses and Paynes), and two couples each. Peter and I invited Cliff and Jean Michelmore and broadcaster David Jacobs and his wife Lyndsay. The Paynes invited Larry and Adrienne Sacking, a super couple in the antiques business, and Simon Roberts, Chairman of Job's Dairy, and his wife Katie. All were asked to come dressed for a banquet, and this they did, magnificently!

I must confess to a heart-stopping moment of pride when we were all eventually seated! The soft glowing candlelight, the gleaming silver and the long rustling silk dresses of the ladies beside our immaculate escorts made quite the most spectacular night my dining room has ever witnessed. And then came the banquet!

As each course made its appearance, Alan gave us a brief history of its origins and of the wine we were drinking – and we listened, spellbound.

First came a cream pea soup, Crème de Pois Nouveaux. This was served at a banquet given on 7 March 1905 at Buckingham Palace in honour of Prince Ferdinand of Bulgaria. It was light, creamy smooth and delicate in taste. A Chassagne Montrachet 1979 served with it was chilled to perfection.

Our second course, said Alan, was featured at a banquet at Windsor Castle on 3 June 1905, and a gasp arose when Côtelette de Saumon à la Montpellier appeared. The tiny cold poached cutlets of salmon sat poised on a silver platter in a sea of creamy green herb butter, and tasted indescribably good.

Our raconteur went on to tell us that our third course was a favourite of King Edward VII who was a renowned shot and very fond of game. Salmis de Faisan was a supreme of pheasant, part roasted and then braised with port and brandy and served on tiny croutons. It was rich, brown and delicious, and with it we drank a smooth Volnay 1979 Louis Latour.

We rested a while then, with tiny dishes of Champagne Sorbet to cleanse the palate. Finally came the great moment for us, as our silky smooth Château Lafite, perfect in temperature, was poured with loving care to accompany the Selle d'Agneau à la Portuguaise. This was another favourite of King Edward, said Alan: saddle of lamb cooked to pinky perfection, garnished with tiny stuffed tomatoes and just a few beautifully cooked vegetables to accompany it.

By now the conversation was sparkling and the atmosphere had mellowed into one of warm embracing friendship. A pause to reflect on what had gone before – and then on to the finale: Crêpes Alexandra, named after King Edward's wife, Alexandra of Denmark. And they were truly perfection in a dessert. Wafer-thin, melt-in-the-mouth crêpes were filled with a poached pear and chestnut purée, rolled up and served hot with tiny sprigs of crystallized mint decorating the plates, and a bottle of Château Roner 1969 Sauternes, sweet and chilled, married perfectly with them.

It was a very special night – a pinnacle of entertaining and a pleasure that I shall always remember. Some time after the dinner party I begged one recipe from Alan and he gave me the **Côtelette de Saumon à la Montpellier**. In the same letter came Coffee Jelly and Hare Pie from *Gunter's Confectioner's Oracle* of 1830! I laughed and loved their strange language, with words like 'decoction' and 'cedratys', but I must confess that I have not, as yet, tried either of them. If any brave reader does, I really would like to hear how they turn out.

These recipes remind me, a little, of a fantastic almond pud we had on a visit to the Algarve some years ago. With us on a long weekend sponsored by American Express was Willie Bauer, Managing Director of the Savoy Hotel, London, an old friend of ours. On the final night of our visit a magnificent pud, moist rather like a roulade but feather-light and rich, appeared on the dinner table. Willie asked for the recipe, and I asked Willie for a copy. This is what he sent me.

Algarve Special
36 eggs
1 kg sugar
800 g nibbed almonds
200 g flour

The method was as for a roulade, the filling was:

1 kg sugar
30 egg yolks
25 cl water

Well, its sheer Mrs Beeton, isn't it, with her 'Take 20 eggs…' Perhaps not one for our book – but you're welcome to try!

FOOD FOR ALL SEASONS

I can never make up my mind whether I prefer summer or winter entertaining, both have so much to commend them. The summers, with casual barbecues, the long light evenings and drinks on the terrace before dinner, the french windows wide open to the sweetly embracing perfumes of the syringa, honeysuckle and night-scented stocks. Or the winters with the curtains drawn fast against the cold, the log fires crackling and the flames leaping up the chimney, throwing dancing patterns against the walls and ceilings.

Because I believe that my guests come to see both of us, not my husband and my back disappearing into the kitchen, I try to devise a meal that needs the minimum of last-minute preparation so that I can be with our guests – and enjoy my pre-dinner drink!

I serve either cold starters or something hot that is just simmering quietly without spoiling until the guests are ready to come to the table. Nothing is worse than a hostess appealing to the company to be seated when one guest is deep into a story that has the whole room engrossed. The flat, collapsed soufflé and her white, agonized face are not the signs of an enjoyable evening.

I often puree vegetables, spinach, swedes, parsnips, peas, carrots, celeriac, almost any you can mention, cooked and popped hot into the blender with a knob of butter, some freshly ground black pepper, maybe some herbs from the garden and a little fresh cream; they are simple to do and look very effective served on the plate. Red cabbage, braised with apple and served with, say, game or pork, is different and colourwise very pretty, as is another of my favourites, tiny French or Kenya beans, left whole, cooked for 8 minutes and, when hot and still crispy, tossed in butter and black pepper.

I tend not to try complicated recipes for Nouvelle Cuisine. I avidly read books about it, but to eat it I prefer to go to a restaurant where the chef has many hands to help him with all the reducing and layering that is involved, plus the time for the delicate presentation which is so much part of its appeal.

For starters try **Insalata dei Funghi** – an interesting mushroom and prawn concoction that I found in the *Telegraph* Colour Magazine some years ago. I think the article was by Denis Curtis, a writer/cook whose work and style I much admire. Another sure-fire winner is Helen Wogan's **Caviar Pie**. It is very simple to do and looks fearfully clever when served cut like a cake with smoked salmon and lemon halves. Many's the happy evening we've spent in their company. Indeed they have one of our Weimaraner pups called, appropriately, Alice.

Terry is godfather to our youngest, Henry, and well I remember the christening in our tiny village church. The Reverend John Bundock was marvellous and coped really well with the unusual congregation of showbiz and family, but his face was a picture when he saw 'Our Tel' striding down the aisle with the baby!

Bruce Forsyth is a Piscean, like my husband. 'Two fish,' they wickedly laugh at each other, 'frantically swimming in opposite directions!' 'Soft, loveable, and useless around the house,' quotes my husband, and that is indeed true enough. Ask him to change a plug and he manages to fuse the entire system. Not that I don't think that now, after all these years, he doesn't trade on it. 'Don't ask me – you know it's bound to end in disaster' is one of his favourite sayings.

Some years ago Bruce spent a weekend with us during the days leading up to Peter's birthday. After he had gone, the 28th of February dawned and the ring of the postman produced a large, long flat parcel. Bemused, Peter opened it to find a piece of hardboard with two kippers, one stapled on each side, nose to tail. The note read: 'From one Pisces to another.' Bruce has always made us laugh, though once the laugh was on him. At the British Open one year, he wanted to be able to follow the golf without being surrounded by fans, so he donned a long mackintosh, a floppy felt hat and dark glasses, and set off. Unbeknown to him, someone in the BBC Television caravan, while slapping him on the back had stuck a large notice on him saying 'This is Bruce Forsyth.' Poor Bruce, everywhere he went he was followed by roars of mirth and leg-pulling. It was over an hour before someone told him what was going on!

The friendship between Bruce and Peter goes back many years, through broken marriages on both sides, through tears, laughter and much happiness, especially since Winnie, Bruce's lovely Puerto Rican wife, produced his first son, J.J., in 1986, after five daughters. Winnie's cooking is very different, much in the style of her own country. Her recipe for **Fried Fish with Puerto Rico Sauce** is lovely; do try it, it's different and easy to do.

David and Lyndsay Jacobs, David of the soft voice and beautiful music programmes, are close friends and we greatly value their friendship. David is always a pleasure to be with, witty, attentive, a self-confessed lover of ladies in the nicest sense and a man of devastating charm to those around him, kept quietly in check by his lovely wife, Lyndsay, who has created with her talent for design and eye for detail a home that is a pleasure to enter.

Peter has known David casually for many years, and I met him purely by chance one day when taking the 9.10 Haslemere to Waterloo train and David got on at Milford Station. I must confess to not instantly recognizing him, and, as many of you might know, the morning commuter trains are full of businessmen who love their *Financial Times*, peer over their glasses at you when you enter the carriage and then resume their reading – all in total reserved silence!

David had mislaid his ticket, and completely disrupted the compartment by standing up and searching his pockets, his briefcase and his overcoat, accompanying this with a worried running commentary. Watching the reaction on the stony faces of the other travellers gave me a fit of the giggles.

At last he gave up the search, deciding he must have left the ticket at Milford. He sat down and peace reigned. It was then I noticed the initials 'D.J.' on his briefcase – and the penny dropped.

As we left the train together at Waterloo I couldn't resist saying to him, 'Lots of people tell my husband how much they enjoy his commentaries, so I would just like to tell you what pleasure you give me with your Saturday and Sunday morning radio programmes.'

'Who is your husband?' said he.

'Peter Alliss,' said I.

He burst into laughter. 'Imagine sitting opposite Peter's wife and not knowing. We've just moved out of London – come to dinner and meet Lyndsay!' We did, and it's been a close friendship ever since.

A request to dine at the Jacobs's house is a pleasure not to be missed, as much for the excellence of Lyndsay's menu as for the minute attention to the smallest details. A simple but perfect steak and kidney is complemented by a table gleaming with highly polished rosy apples in a woven rush basket, with arrangements of dried flowers, herbs, wild flowers and nuts, and always an assembled company which sets the conversation sparkling. Well remembered is the summer alfresco luncheon some two years ago held on a perfect July day on the lawn of their newly acquired country cottage. Trestle tables were covered by gleaming white cloths and white daisies were everywhere: on the table, on the cloths, on the china, on the napkins, and fresh Michaelmas daisy heads pushed through the cut-out lids of succulently sweet ice-cold Ogen melons. It was a day to remember; one of those days one pulls out of the memory bank in years to come.

Lyndsay's **Pea Soup** is well worth trying, filling and simple to make. I too now make it for Boxing Day, to go with the cold meats.

There have been so many delicious meals over the years, so many recipes begged after a particularly special evening. Pat Wood's marvellous **Stilton Pâté** always reminds me of a summer luncheon in the peace and tranquillity of their forest home near Liphook, in Hampshire. Jan Lack, apologizing for the lack of decoration in their new home near Midhurst and serving us a magnificent **Crab Mousse** that had everyone assembled asking for seconds. Caroline Harvey, a special lady who expertly runs the restaurants at British Car Auctions, Camberley; at her home one night we ate a simple supper after a long hard day, consisting of large moist slices of smoked salmon, simply filled with a mixture of prawns, some cream and a touch of horseradish, rolled up, popped onto crunchy chopped iceberg lettuce and decorated with a spoonful of mock caviar and lots of chopped parsley and lemon.

I am, I suppose, a believer in good quality above all, and super-freshness. Living in the country, we are so lucky with lots of 'pick-your-own' fruit and vegetable places, good local bakeries and, above all, our local farm run by Peter and Celia Haines, along with various members of their family.

One of my children's greatest pleasures, and indeed one of mine, are the spring mornings spent watching Celia's lambs. Sitting on bales of straw in the pens with these adorable babes gambolling around their woolly mums and watching Celia bottle-feed the weaker ones, has to be one of life's great lessons on simplicity and uncomplicated pleasure.

Their superb prize Jersey herd produces the cream for ice creams and sorbets, and the thickest freshest Jersey cream to be found. Delicious. No wonder we are all fighting the flab!

CHAPTER EIGHT

TRAVELS OVERSEAS

UNITED STATES

IN MY EARLIER DAYS life was by no means always champagne and caviar! I well remember one of my first trips to America. It is clear in my memory because I travelled on my own to join my husband who was already in San Diego to cover a golf tournament for ABC Television. As I sat in the lounge at Heathrow Airport feeling very grand, and vaguely apprehensive about being on my own, but avidly watching the bustle that is part of any major airport, it was impossible to miss a tall, somewhat thin young lady, distinctive in her floppy large-brimmed hat, gloves and tight skirt, revealing yards of leg. She was obviously in a hurry, getting close to panic and totally disrupted the First Class lounge. I remember thinking, 'I wonder which flight she's on.'

Some twenty minutes later I was to find out. Escorted by some kind BEA gentleman and shown to my seat (it was my first time ever in First Class and I was sure that every bit of pleasure showed on my face!), I was just savouring the moment when, you've guessed it, she came charging up the aisle, tripped, lost her hat over her eyes and nearly ended up in my lap. Her name, she said, was Carol. Wasn't everything too dreadful! She'd lost her hand luggage, her finger was in plaster and her husband was meeting her when, and if, we ever arrived in Los Angeles (she was, she explained 'dreadfully accident-prone').

By now I was totally speechless and was to remain so as she never paused to draw breath. Her finger was a result of tumbling from top to bottom of the curved staircase leading from the upstairs lounge on a Jumbo aircraft. She had missed her footing, slipped and, in reaching for the rail, caught her wedding ring on the wrought iron and almost severed her finger. Two of her four days in London had been spent in hospital and she was now homeward-bound – without her hand luggage. To date, she'd had two emergency landings, flown through an electric storm, and had accidents too numerous to recount. Wasn't she lucky, she said, brightly and loudly, knocking her coffee all over my knees, to be still here! Never was I so glad to arrive safely at LA, to transfer to United Airlines and to say goodbye to my companion. I often wonder whether she managed to survive the years to come!!

Some time later, arriving at San Diego, tired but delighted to see my husband's face and our hosts, Tom and Callie Crow, I was taken straight out to dine with their friends and had my first taste of lobster tails and a succulent Crab Mould which we often make now. Since then, I have often made the trip to the United States and been lucky enough to make many friends, eaten both excellent food and some indifferent stuff – and I jump at the chance to return whenever possible.

The Lodge at Pebble Beach in California is high on my list of favourite places. When I first went there some seventeen years ago, it was owned by the huge Del Monte fruit corporation and known as Del Monte Lodge. Situated on the famous Monterey Peninsula, it was virtually a private estate with a spectacular 17-mile drive around its perimeter. The golf course has staged many of America's top golfing events, including the Open Championship, and was, for many years, the home of the Bing Crosby Tournament.

A mere skip and a jump away are the spectacular and very exclusive Cypress Point and the equally dramatic Spyglass Hill. Truly a Mecca for golf lovers. To me, it was the sheer pleasure of standing on our balcony watching the colourful scene of the golfers playing and the sun sparkling on the water, the seals basking on the rocks, rolling in the waves, splashing on their backs and clapping their flippers in fun. And if you were very lucky you might see the spouting jets of water from the whales migrating across the bay.

Many of the rooms had open fire-places with well-stocked baskets of eucalyptus logs. There can be few more romantic settings than dinner for two overlooking the bay, on a late summer evening, the fire burning and the sweet aroma of eucalyptus floating into the silvery moonlight as it traces a path across the sea.

Over the years I have collected many recipes from the marvell-ously hospitable people who have been kind enough to entertain us and show us around. After my first trip to Los Angeles Open Market, my fascination with cheesecakes was born. It is a market unlike any other I have come across – just acres of stalls, restaurants, shops and entertainment. Never will I forget my first sight of the stall selling cheesecakes, either whole or a slice on a plate to eat there and then. They must have had a choice of over thirty and I could easily have tried them all! I was hard pushed not to spend the next five days exploring the market instead of being on the golf course; only sheer willpower – and my husband, who's bigger than me – kept me away.

After that day I talked to my guide, a lovely lady called Mrs Johnson, whose son, Sal, worked as a 'gofer' for ABC. She gave me a recipe for **American Gelatin Cheesecake** which is huge and deliciously gooey, will serve up to 18 people and can be made without worry the day before it is needed.

San Francisco is traditionally a magical tourist 'must'. My own memories are just as special – but very different! I drove across Golden Gate Bridge in an open-topped car in the morning sunshine with one Terry Jastrow, a Director of Golf with ABC Television and a great friend. He is devastatingly handsome ('Horribly slim,' says my just slightly overweight husband), and all three of us were suffering somewhat from the party the night before.

We drove for brunch to a hotel overlooking the bay that is famed for its menu. Terry ordered Eggs Benedict, fresh orange juice and coffee all round. The eggs looked marvellous. Peter had a manful try at his, I sat in queasy silence, contemplating the spectacular view, drinking my coffee and wishing I felt well enough to eat what, I was sure, were perfect Eggs Benedict.

I have lived most of my adult life as a golfer's wife, and learnt early in my marriage to take, and appreciate, the times we get together especially as they seem so few in the busy golfing calendar. And so the warm sunny day Peter and I had to ourselves to explore San Francisco – and in particular Fisherman's Wharf – was and is a very special day in my memory.

We came across a pet shop quite by chance which was full of the most glorious parrots (and I have a passion for these birds). The owner, seeing this, tried desperately to persuade my husband that it was a cheap and easy job to ship one home. He failed. There too we saw for the first time the incredible street performers and stood there wide-eyed, watching their antics. I loved it all, the comedians, the puppet shows, the actors, and most of all I loved the sheer exuberance of it all.

Then we wandered around the boats and the old ships moored by the harbour side, marvelling at the old iron guns, the size of the huge wooden spars and the obvious simplicity and hardness of the life a sailor must have experienced some 150 years ago.

There were masses of tiny boutiques mixed in with the bigger shops, the contents of which differed so greatly from our own. The pendant, hand-painted, that my husband bought me as a souvenir is still a very treasured possession. We had lunch in a tree-shaded open-air restaurant where we could sit lazily sipping a glass of cold wine and watch the cosmopolitan world walk by. The dessert we chose that day was a **Soured Cream Flan**, light, creamy, with a sharp tang that always reminds me of our glorious day. I begged the recipe from the bustling owner and managed to write it down as he gabbled out the method; the one I make today is a fair copy!

The Dinah Shore Tournament was played for many years at Mission Hills in Palm Springs. This was a ladies' event, one of the most prestigious in the United States, and at that time was organized and sponsored by the giant Colgate Corporation under the watchful eye of David Foster, one of the world's greatest golf enthusiasts.

Palm Springs over 50 years ago was little more than a sleeping desert village mainly inhabited by Indians and a few hardy prospectors, but in the last 30 years it has grown to enormous proportions. When the Ryder Cup matches were played at Thunderbird Golf Club in 1955 there were less than a handful of courses in the area – now there are close on 100.

It has a marvellous climate, hot in summer, very dry and warm in winter, and because fashionable as a retirement area it soon acquired the affectionate nickname 'God's Waiting Room' as the residents seemed to live to a ripe old age. Sadly, with the advent of irrigation, watering, lakes and many many swimming pools being built, the very air that was so dry is now becoming much more humid.

On my first visit, in the Seventies, we stayed at Palm Springs Hotel. A good friend persuaded me that what I, and my body, needed most was a visit to the famous hot springs bath house. Natural hot springs of mineral water bubble up from the earth, full of natural goodness. Afterwards you have a massage guaranteed to make you feel on top of the world. With some trepidation I agreed. As we moved slowly from one room to another I must confess that slowly stifling in steam is not my favourite occupation. But I loved the Eucalyptus Room with its menthyl steam and I could have stayed much longer than the alloted 20 minutes in the hot tub with its strangely smelling, swirling water that somehow made you physically aware of the tensions creeping out of your body.

The next bit was something of a shock. As we stood against a wall, the attendant hosed us down with a very strong jet of water – it gave me the giggles as I felt vaguely like an elephant at the zoo! A large Slavic lady then collected me and my towel and took me to the massage room where, for the next 30 minutes, I had the most thorough and expert massage. After half an hour's doze, I felt as if I was walking on air, and when finally I was reunited with my husband we indulged in coffee and a slice of **Carrot Cake** to celebrate. The cake was superb and started me on a quest for a recipe. I have eaten different varieties of it all over the world and my present recipe is the closest to that slice at Palm Springs.

HONG KONG

It never fails to amaze me how small the world is becoming with the increase and availability of air travel and charter holidays. I went to Hong Kong for the first time some ten years ago. Before the trip I was bubbling with excitement because for years a visit had been top of my list of ambitions. The first day there, I left our hotel for a walk to explore, with Peter's instructions ringing in my ears: not to go too far and not to get lost!

Wandering along, taking in the people, the colour, the bustle, the heat reflecting off the dusty pavements and the noise and clamour from the harbour, I was lost in my own thoughts when I suddenly bumped into someone. Turning automatically to apologize, I came face to face with my oldest girlfriend's husband! We burst into laughter and ended up having coffee in the Mandarin Hotel!

I loved Hong Kong, for me it was a magical city with its extremes of rich and poor. Masses of export shops sold jade, pearls and diamonds, while at the same time washing was strung across the streets, forming huge colourful banners everywhere, and seaweed was laid out in the streets to dry in the sun. The ferry boats busily chugged across the harbour – and oh, the shops. What temptation for a mere mortal! Silks by the roll in every colour, hue and design imaginable, some already with matching clutch handbags. A dress, handmade to measure, took two days, a raw silk shirt 24 hours; shoes, bags, belts, nothing was impossible.

As guests one night of Kim and Lily Hall we had a meal that is forever emblazoned on our memories! Kim, who sadly died two years ago, was a fascinating man, a World War II fighter pilot who had been stationed in Hong Kong, came to love it, married a Hong Kong Chinese girl and took up residence. He quickly saw the possibilities of sports agencies in the Far East and was there at the beginning of the boom of sport in Asia. A small rotund man, always laughing, explosive, hospitable to a fault, it was always a pleasure to see him and his lovely wife Lily.

One evening, during the Hong Kong Golf Championship, a party of us went out for dinner, not to one of the usual restaurants or hotels, but through the back streets to the Suzy Wong district of the city. It was a small unprepossessing place, reached via two flights of bare wooden stairs, and there I had one of the finest meals I have ever eaten. We sat at a huge circular table with a revolving centrepiece onto which each course was placed and the centrepiece slowly spun so that everyone could help themselves as each dish reached their place. The lightest, crispiest appetizers, giant butterfly prawns, squid, delicately flavoured soup in tiny porcelain bowls, wafer-thin strips of perfect beef, beansprouts, seaweed and other vegetables that I didn't recognize. Peking Duck with its crispy skin, moist tender flesh, spring onions and a rich dark sweet soy sauce, all wrapped in a type of thin oatmeal pancake. For me the *pièce de résistance* was the main fish dish, a whole white fish, rather like a sea bass, cooked in a flour and water paste case which, when it came to the table, huge, very hot and pale brown, was cracked open to reveal the most succulent, steaming, gently flavoured flesh imaginable.

The meal moved slowly to a climax and we realized we had been sitting there savouring course after course for over four hours! It would have to count, for me, as one of the 'great meals'.

Back in England I experimented with paste, none too successfully, and then moved back to pastry. Nowadays I wrap many things in flaky pastry because the children love it: fish, steamed and skinned with sliced tomatoes; chicken pieces, fillet of pork and fillet of lamb all taste delicious with chopped mushrooms, onions, pâté, apples or prunes popped inside the pastry for added flavour.

FRENCH LEAVE

Travelling has taken us to so many beautiful places in the world. A particular favourite with me is La Baule in Brittany, France. Some ten years ago Peter and his partner were designing and building the golf course there and we stayed several times as a family at the Hermitage Hotel, part of the Groupe Barrière and ably managed by Gerald and

Andrea Mauget. We became good friends and looked forward to our visits with a great sense of pleasure. I love the Normandy-Brittany coast of France, maybe for its rugged coastline and maybe for its lack of sophistication, also for its easy-going hospitable people and particularly for the abundance of glorious fish and shellfish which are prepared and served to an exceptionally high standard. You can find them in every little restaurant from the humblest pavement café to the grandest hotel. If you have never tasted Matelote d'Anguilles à la Bourgeoise, a marvellous fish stew which can include anything, in addition to the basic eels, from carp or pike to any fish from the catch of the day – you've never lived!!

In the early Seventies, after a golf tournament at La Manga in Spain, Peter and I made the return journey by car through France, up through the Bordeaux country to Le Havre. We decided to stay over-night en route, and about 5.30 pm I suggested we should start looking for a hostelry as we were then passing several that looked inviting. 'No,' said my husband, 'we will push on for another hour.' And so we did, but then of course there was nothing. I sank into my seat getting crosser and crosser while he grew quieter and quieter. At last, we came to a village. 'Must be somewhere here,' said he. Two hotels – both full; on we went. At 8.30, in total silence, we passed a roadside inn. It looked shabby, certainly nothing special, but it was open! In desperation Peter said, 'We'll have a drink and see what it's like.' We went in and ended up staying for a meal which was local, seasonal and quite superb: oysters in abundance, veal as tender as butter, a farmhouse plum tart, Le Pruné, made from those dark almost purple plums and served warm with thick cream. And just when I thought I couldn't eat another mouthful, tiny local goat's cheeses were brought to the table with another carafe of the local wine, compliments of the house!

Some time later, after several coffees and brandies and much joking and laughter with the locals who had come in for their evening drinks, we wandered off to bed. The least said about our room the better! Suffice to say, it was clean, spartan and small with the strangest loo I have ever seen in my life! The next morning, woken by the cows and the early hotel bustle, we had a hearty breakfast of café au lait, rolls and plum jam, and were on our way. We left with the friendly faces of our hosts smiling, and a memory of a never-to-be-repeated night.

ANTIGUA

Summer holidays have never been a big thing in the Alliss household, mainly because of Peter's heavy work schedule from May to October. I take the children skiing in the Easter holidays, and once a year at the end of January or in early February, Peter and I head for the Caribbean.

Believe it or not, the golf clubs come too. Our destination is Antigua and the Half Moon Bay Hotel, and we go there with several good friends who enjoy both sunshine and golf. We give ourselves three weeks of no papers, no television, no phones, just sun, sea and balmy romantic nights under heavily star-laden skies. Three weeks of fun and laughter, attempting unsuccessfully to windsurf, days out on the old pirate ship sailing across the coral reefs to the deep purple lagoons with silky white sandy beaches within lazy swimming distance. Three weeks of not bothering to do my hair, except to wash and dry it in the sun, of seeing my face in the mirror slowly turning a golden brown and freckles emerging from my pale winter skin. Three weeks of eating fruit in glorious abundance at every meal.

The very word fruit conjures up pictures of fist-sized avacados growing in the tiny gardens lining the roads, of fresh lemons, limes and oranges, still green in their freshness, of pinky yellow mangoes, of coconuts hanging in clusters under the swaying palm trees on the plantations. Of pineapple so fresh that the smell is tantalizingly good, of paw-paws, bananas, plantains and balloon-shaped breadfruits hanging pendulously from their trees. The island is green and lush, the Antiguans friendly and hospitable, and it is always a pleasure to return for they greet you like an old friend.

Not far from the hotel, by car, is Nelson's Harbour, slowly being renovated with loving care to its original glory. For more than 100 years, from the late 17th century until well into the 18th – the Caribbean was the scene of a giant struggle for naval supremacy among the European powers. Sugar was the great prize, in total terms more valuable even than gold and silver, and the Royal Navy needed secure bases from which to sail with their precious cargo. Port Royal in Jamaica was chosen as one base, and English Harbour in Antigua was another. By 1723 the harbour was in regular use. Construction began to fortify it and raise the barracks on Shirley Heights, named after General Thomas Shirley who arrived in 1781 as Governor, and who felt that in those times of unrest English Harbour was vulnerable to attack from the French.

It was during this time that young Captain Horatio Nelson, aged just 26 years, arrived in command of the frigate *Boreas*. He was not a popular man when he insisted on enforcing the Navigation Act, passed in London and quietly flouted by the Antiguan merchants, but he did see that the work at English Harbour continued, and as a result it is known today as Nelson's Dockyard.

At the beginning of this century the dockyard was abandoned by the Royal Navy and remained in a sad state of decay until an organization called the Friends of English Harbour was formed in 1951 with the idea of developing the historic site so that it could be used as a centre for ocean-going yachts. Nowadays, as they take a leisurely stroll in the sunshine even the most hardened tourist cannot fail to be moved with nostalgia. The wooden frame mansion in which Nelson was billeted is now a museum filled with letters, commands from the Royal Court, uniforms, silver, Nelson's four-poster bed, and many letters from his love, Lady Emma Hamilton. The Engineer's Workshop has been skilfully converted into the Admiral's Inn where one can sit in peace, overlooking the dock entrance with its huge stone pillars that marked the old boathouse. Gazing across the water to the hillside opposite, you can see Clarence House, the home of Nelson's friend the Duke of Clarence; this is the house where Princess Margaret and Tony Armstrong-Jones spent their honeymoon. Higher up the hill on Shirley Heights the former barracks have been restored as a museum, and perched at the very top is a pleasant little bar and restaurant with panoramic views of the mountains, the sea and the yacht-filled harbour.

To stand quietly, drink in hand, watching the spectacularly beautiful sunsets, is truly one of life's miracles, especially when one is lucky enough to witness the Blue Streak, the flash that comes at the precise moment the sun drops over the horizon. Bathed in the rosy hue of the falling sun, high above the world, it's all too easy to go back in time and imagine how everything must have looked when Nelson first watched the same sunset.

We often stop for a morning drink at the Copper Lumber Store and in the cool interior our host, The Commander, will insist that we try a Commander's Special, a good measure of medium white rum such as Cavalier, freshly squeezed lime juice, topped up with soda and a touch of Angostura Bitters, ice and a slice of fresh lime. It slips down all too easily. The food in the island is delicious, often spicy with a tremendous variety of dishes, a natural mingling of French and African cuisines with touches of British, Chinese, Indian and Portuguese thrown in.

Marinating is probably the essence of Caribbean cooking and

spices are chosen for each dish with special care. Soups are greatly loved and famous above all is Callaloo Soup, very traditional, enormously popular, and delicious to eat.

Fish is still the staple food in the island. I personally love their flying fish, often served with a sauce of tomatoes, garlic, oil, onion, fresh herbs and lime juice. Chicken is also a local favourite, often reared in the yard years ago but now, sadly, more likely to be kept in captivity and fattened with imported feed.

I like chicken fricasseed with brown sugar, oil, onions and celery or curried with cumin seed and curry powder, lime, thyme and garlic and served with light and fluffy steamed rice. My favourite, because I love coriander, is Coriander Chicken, easy to do using chicken pieces.

We also love our barbecues on the beach, the food cooked to perfection on halved oil drums over a fire of palm fronds, and the meal finished with Coconut Ice Cream which, somehow, never tastes the same back at home. But there are so many lovely tastes to try at home, and adapt. We are lucky now in England that more tropical fruits are widely available to us: prickly pears, ugly fruits, passion fruits, kiwis and mangoes amongst many. All make superb sorbets and the humble fruit salad can never be called humble again.

Mango is the fruit I perhaps use most. I chop it into salads, sliced and mixed with fresh cream, and it is delicious rolled into an orange-flavoured roulade; pureed, it can be transformed into soufflés and whisper-light mousses, and it is a winner with chicken or veal. Shellfish blend beautifully with it, too; try fresh crab, mixed with creamy home-made mayonnaise and mango slices for a starter, or prawns, mango and melon, chilled, mixed with a vinaigrette dressing and served on a bed of radicchio salad and lots of sprigs of fresh mint. It really is such an adaptable fruit. Kiwi too, thanks to good old M & S, is much loved: I serve them in a roulade, skinned and chopped with fresh whipped cream, flavoured with Grand Marnier, pecan kernals and fresh oranges, sliced, de-pithed and chopped and drained on kitchen paper to remove the excess juice.

This year in Antigua we were joined by a new couple, a golf-addict husband and a sun-worshipper wife – they fitted in beautifully! Idly talking about recipes on the beach one day, Cheryl said she had a super recipe for **Passion Fruit Mousse**. A month later, back home in the cold and damp of late February, they came for dinner – a sort of photographic reunion – and Cheryl arrived armed with a tub of her mousse. It was delicious; one taste and I am immediately transferred back to our beach, the scorching sun and the lapping sea at our feet!

CHAPTER NINE

TODAY

TRAVEL HAS PLAYED A MAJOR PART in my life and I still, to this day, get a sense of excitement before flying, but the glitter of long distance travel can wear thin when you are stuck miles from home in some dark, deserted airport at 3 o'clock in the morning due to fog, or half-frozen for six hours due to the heating system 'temporarily' malfunctioning; and the nagging fear when an engine fails, that perhaps one might not make it to see loved ones again, is not a pleasant feeling.

But I still marvel at the sheer magnificent power of a 747 rushing along the runway to climb weightlessly into the clouds. Indeed, the appeal became so strong two years ago, thanks to the influence of two men, David Wickins, and Alan Curtis, that I screwed up my courage, booked into Blackbushe School of Flying at Camberley, Surrey, and buried myself into learning the science of flight.

I studied Air Law, Navigation, Meteorology and Aircraft Technical Knowledge. In due course, after many hard hours of work, frequently wondering about my sanity and why I wanted to fly, I passed and obtained my PPL (Private Pilot's Licence). The total thrill of being able to fly, alone, at 3,000 feet on a perfectly clear day away from the hurly-burly of everyday domesticity, is absolutely glorious.

Learning to fly was such a new experience. As a 'mere' female in a very male-orientated world, it took quite a lot of guts and talking to myself to keep going after the first few sorties into a flying club that seemed packed with men in denims and flying jackets all talking knowledgeably about the pilot static system and aerodynamic forces! Trying to grasp these new concepts, to look as if at least some of it made sense, then returning home in a state of total panic: I'll never get the hang of this! Only pride, and a fiercely independent streak, kept me going through those early weeks.

My instructor was a quiet, competent young man called Peter Diggin who, I'm sure, picked the short straw, got the lady and had to put up with quite a bit of leg-pulling. But he was very patient and we became good friends – we certainly had a lot of laughs! In due course he managed to push all the relevant and necessary facts into my head and the denim-clad men in the club turned out to be a marvellous bunch, very supportive and quick to offer help with the exam work.

And the laughs we had when several of us were waiting to do our cross-country qualifying flights – the quiet trepidation when the day dawned fair and clear and it was off, solo, on the first leg to Staverton, then on to Oxford and back to base – and the enormous relief and story-telling when one got safely home again, papers stamped, without getting lost. I cannot think of anything that has given me a greater sense of fulfilment and was so worth all the hard work involved.

I do realize that I have been extraordinarily lucky in having a husband who has allowed me my freedom to have a go. There must have been times he worried, but he always encouraged me and I think he now takes a quiet pride in his wife's achievements. My fellow-fliers and I have formed our Monday Club. We try to fly each Monday, weather permitting, sharing the flying and the costs. Over the months we have probably visited most of the small airfields in the country.

And so, here we are in the late Eighties, settled in Surrey, the children growing up and my 'little one' just started at school. My garden, under Neil's watchful eye, is a picture of changing moods and colour, filled with fruit trees, vegetables and flowers. I sometimes feel that in my old age I could easily become a fanatical gardener, and the old housewifery tasks of bottling and jam-making hold a considerable appeal. Our own harvest of apples, plums, damsons and pears is an added bonus.

I make only two jams, strawberry and blackcurrant, as no-one eats the others and I freeze large amounts of pureed apple for the winter months. We all love Apple Charlottes and Crumbles, Apple Strudels and Cobblers, and have you tried poaching whole peeled pears with a vanilla stick in syrup? When tender, cool and drain, and wrap in a shortcrust pastry coat, leaving the stalk sticking out, and cook until golden brown in a moderate oven. When the pastry is golden-brown, pour a little melted crabapple jelly or quince jelly into the inside down via the stalk, and serve piping hot with thick Jersey cream. Crème Brûlée, made with peeled and halved seedless grapes, popped into the bottom of the dish, and tiny sweet, deep-orange clementines peeled and segmented and dipped into chocolate – delicious.

Christmas is a traditional feast in our household, as in most families, I suspect. Now that two children are old enough to come with me to the midnight service at our local St John's Church in Churt, I find great pleasure from the service that, for me, is the start of Christmas. My memories always go back to my first Christmas spent away from home in Lausanne, Switzerland. The snow that Christmas Eve was thick and crunchy underfoot, the world was quiet and still on our way to church, a crispy cold night with a clear sky ablaze with a thousand stars proclaiming Christ's birth. But nothing prepared me for the sight inside the church when the huge wooden doors swung open to the warmth and light within. A tree stretched up to the rafters, covered from top to toe with fresh oranges on golden strings and ablaze with the light from hundreds of real white candles at the tips of every branch. It was so staggeringly beautiful, and its total simplicity summed up the perfection of Christ, His birth, and Christmas.

Christmas is a time for memories, of scents of pine and baking fruit cake, of little children and their wide-eyed wonderment, for 'grown-up' children to rediscover that there is still a miracle working for us all and, maybe, like me, you too resent the increasing commercialization of it all. I love the routine of making the cake, and the children wait for the night we make the mincemeat. The recipe is handed down from my maternal great grandmother, and she also had one for Lemon Curd that was mouth-wateringly good, but it sadly got lost when she died.

We all follow the old superstition that one should eat 12 mince pies between Christmas and New Year to ensure 12 happy months ahead. Some years ago I found a recipe for Royal Mince Pie said to be 200 years old; the results were delicious. We eat them as they come out of the Aga, with burn fingers and lots of squeals – a wonderful treat.

Christmas when I was a child meant home-made truffles – a treat upon which my sister and I spent hours of concentration. With hindsight, it was probably engineered by our mother to keep us out from under her feet and quiet.

Christmas today is not a lot different, except that I confess to a passion for Christmas trees and I rush out when my husband is away for the day and buy three. Presented with a *fait accompli*, there's not much he can do about it. One little one is for Henry, in the playroom, covered in lights, chocolate baubles, tiny Santas and home-made decorations. These are cut out and coloured with loving care, or glued with tubes of coloured sparkle, by Henry and his nanny, 'Moose' (Melanie Peereboom).

The second tree is in the dining room, placed in the French windows and aglow with silver and red baubles and all red lights, a set that I inherited from my father which must be all of 16 years old. Each year I cross my fingers and pray that they will survive another year. Against the deep rose-red curtains, the glow of the tree and the candles on the table fill me with a deep sense of peace and a strange feeling of that 'orange tree' in Lausanne. The third tree goes in the drawing room, and is the one we pile all our presents under – colourful and covered by all the bits and novelties we have collected throughout a lifetime of Christmases. Tinsel, baubles, angels, a star on the top. When all the preparations are finally done, it is here that the magic of Christmas begins.

Because I am a workaholic, I find it very difficult to switch off and do nothing – I'm already looking to the next challenge. I confess to having a powerful urge to do a parachute jump with the Red Devils for one of my charities (it's the one time my husband has been less than enthusiastic!), and I would dearly love to visit Australia and New Zealand. Peter has been visiting both countries since as far back as 1965 and is always glowing in praise. Australia – the handsome city of Melbourne, the marvellous climate, the mixture of peoples and cultures and the cosmopolitan feel of the place. The hustle and bustle of Sydney, the architecture and everywhere the welcome and friendliness. New Zealand – unspoilt, warm, friendly and, as yet, underdeveloped – many say it is like Britain was in the Twenties and Thirties.

I have a desire to start a business – that perhaps will be my horizon for 1988. I'm very superstitious and the number 8 rules my life: table numbers, plane seats, it's amazing how often it crops up – and who knows what '88 will hold in store!

I have been so very fortunate with my life until now, with my husband, my family and our many good and dear friends. I find a quiet satisfaction and immense pleasure in entertaining, in producing a well balanced meal, and a table to do it justice. I don't expect to set the world on fire with exotic dishes and elaborate menus, simply to please my husband and our friends and to send our guests home with pleasant memories of a well-cooked meal, convivial company, a warm atmosphere and a feeling of well-being. Fresh, well prepared food, fresh herbs where possible, delicate flavourings and simplicity are the key; no panic, just a lot of pleasure. My husband says that in golfing parlance I'm about a steady 5 handicapper, but with a smile and a twinkle in his eye he adds that I have been known to cook to scratch!

Recipes

RECIPE NOTES

MEASURES

Unless otherwise stated, all measures for tbsp, tsp, etc., are level, and a cup is an average English teacup.

FLOUR

Unless otherwise stated, this means plain flour.

PASTRY

As a guide to how much Shortcrust Pastry you will need, 10 oz (275 g) is enough to line a 9 in (23 cm) flan case or top a 2 pt (1.1 l) pie dish. Use the following ingredients:

8 oz (225 g) flour
½ tsp salt
2 oz (50 g) butter
2 oz (50 g) lard
2–3 tbsp cold water

For Sweet Shortcrust Pastry, used for sweet tarts and flans, add 1 oz (25 g) sugar to the ingredients above.

WINES

For my cooking I keep a bottle each of cheapish red and white wine, a bottle of Spanish brandy and a bottle of Marsala.

BEURRE MANIÉ

This is a liaison of butter and flour mixed to a paste and used to thicken sauces, soups or stews. Stir the mixture bit by bit into the cooked dish, and bring back to the boil, stirring until the required thickness is reached.

BAIN MARIE

This is a shallow open tin, half-filled with water and used to prevent dishes such as egg custards and creams from overheating during cooking.

BASIC FRENCH VINAIGRETTE

To make ⅓ pt (185 ml), use the following ingredients:

2 tbsp white wine vinegar
8 tbsp olive oil
1 clove garlic, put through press
1 tsp Dijon mustard
salt, freshly ground black pepper

Put everything together in a screwtop jar and shake well. To vary the formula, try one of these:

Add 2 tsp of caster sugar to the basic recipe.
Try using sunflower oil; this will give you a lighter dressing.
Add a good tbsp chopped herbs for extra flavouring.

Mango Soup
Insalata dei Funghi
Mushrooms Crème Fraîche

SOUPS AND STARTERS

This is always the point of the evening that I love. The frantic last minute rush is over, my guests comfortably established with their drinks, the house warm and friendly, fires roaring in the winter, or French windows open to the terrace and the sweet summer evening smell of stocks and jasmine. The table set and the flowers to my satisfaction, I have time to just stand and view the awaiting table, cold starters in position and just inviting admiration. Cold starters are the obvious answer, cleverly decorated, but hot or cold soups are easy and quick to serve. The following are some of our favourites.

CLAUDINE'S CARROT SOUP

(SERVES 6–8)

I first tasted this soup at The Windmills, high on the Sussex Downs, the home of Claudine and Henry Longhurst.

1 lb (450 g) finely diced onions
2 oz (50 g) butter
2 lb (900 g) carrots (old ones have more flavour)
1 pt (575 ml) chicken stock
½ pt (275 ml) cream, single or double
seasonings
croutons
6–8 tsp cream
parsley, chopped

Cullen Skink Soup

Cook onion in butter until soft and transparent, add sliced carrots, stock, cream and seasonings and simmer very slowly until cooked. (With my Aga I cook this overnight.) Put into blender and liquidize until smooth. Check flavouring and thin down with milk or stock. Serve hot with croutons, a spoonful of cream and chopped fresh parsley.

HAM AND PEA SOUP

(SERVES 4–6)

We have many friends in the New Forest area of Hampshire/Dorset due to Peter spending most of his early life as a professional at Ferndown and Parkstone Golf Clubs. Dr John

Mason, a dentist, and his equally qualified dentist wife Flo, have remained close friends through all our moves up and down the country. We both love visiting their peaceful turn-of-the-century home set on the edge of the forest, near picturesque Burley. This soup is for me a must on a cold winter's day. It is, says Flo, a very cheap and cheerful dish for a shooting lunch, when the menfolk come home covered in glory and mud and clutching their birds.

1 medium forehock of green bacon (soak for 24 hours in 2 changes of cold water)
12 oz (350 g) marrowfat peas (soaked according to instructions on the packet)
1 large Spanish onion
freshly ground black pepper

Put the ham into a large earthenware dish. Wash the soaked peas and add to ham. Chop onion and add to dish plus black pepper. Put in sufficient water to just cover the ham. Bring slowly to the boil and cook with a lid on for at least 4–5 hours, until the peas have broken down and the ham has started to fall off the bone. Serve from the pot with lots of black pepper, hot crusty bread and, of course, chunks of ham – plus a glass of good red plonk.

QUICK BEETROOT SOUP

(SERVES 6)

Not exactly an authentic Bortsch but a good standby, quick to make and delicious served piping hot with cream and chives.

1 lb (450 g) tin beetroot, undrained
¾ pt (425 ml) milk
1 stick celery, sliced
1 good slice onion
salt to taste
cream
chives, finely chopped

Blend, in a mixer or Magimix, beetroot, milk, celery, onion and salt for a good 45 seconds and heat until piping hot. Serve topped with a swirl of cream and a good sprinkling of chives.

PEA SOUP

(SERVES 6)

Lyndsay Jacobs, who gave me this recipe, says they always have this soup before 'the cold' on Boxing Day, served piping hot and with baskets of heart croutons on the table.

1 bunch spring onions, chopped
2 slices ham, chopped
2 oz (50 g) butter
2 lb (900 g) packet frozen peas
1 lettuce heart, chopped
handful fresh mint, chopped
1½ pt (850 ml) chicken stock, made with stock cube
1 tbsp caster sugar
salt, black pepper to taste
cream
croutons

Gently fry onion and ham in a little butter until tender, add all other ingredients and simmer for 30 minutes. Blend in the liquidizer until fairly smooth; we like it thick, but if not to your taste add more stock. Serve cold in summer with a swirl of cream and croutons cut with a 'heart' cutter.

CHESTNUT SOUP

(SERVES 6–8)

One of my Christmas favourites. In Yorkshire we always had up to 40 for lunch on Boxing Day and this soup is easy to make, delicious and filling.

2 oz (50 g) butter

3 sticks celery, chopped

1 medium onion, chopped

1 lb (450 g) chestnut purée unsweetened

1½ pt (850 ml) chicken stock

salt, pepper

1 oz (25 g) butter

1 oz (25 g) flour

cream

croutons

Melt the butter, add celery and onion, cover and sweat until soft and transparent. Blend in the chestnut purée and stock, bring to the boil and simmer for 30 minutes. Put through the blender and season. Thicken, if you prefer a thicker soup, with a beurre manié*, made by mixing the flour into the melted butter and adding it gently, bit by bit, to the soup, stirring all the time. Serve with a swirl of cream and croutons.

* See notes on page 80.

MANGO SOUP

(SERVES 6)

I love the taste of mangoes and am always looking for new ways of serving them. This soup is, to my mind, delicious when served very cold on a hot summer evening.

2 medium ripe mangoes

1 cucumber, unpeeled and rough chopped

juice of 2 limes or lemons

salt to taste

½ pt (275 ml) lightly whipped double cream

lemon peel

mint, finely chopped

Scoop the flesh out from the mangoes and put in the blender with the cucumber, lime juice and a little salt. Remove and combine with the cream. Chill well. This is a thick, fruity soup, and a little is very filling. Sprinkle with finely grated lemon peel and finely chopped fresh mint before serving.

CHILLED CUCUMBER AND WATERCRESS SOUP

(SERVES 6)

This soup always reminds me of Spain – and a little bistro we used frequently during the summers of '84 and '85. Typically Spanish, they loved children and our older two used to run around the grounds playing hide and seek under our watchful eyes, whilst Henry slumbered peacefully in his Moses basket by the

table. This was the special 'house'
soup.

1 oz (25 g) butter
1 small onion, chopped
2 potatoes, peeled and diced
1 cucumber, peeled and cut in 1 in (2.5 cm) pieces
salt and pepper
1 pt (575 ml) chicken stock
½ pt (275 ml) creamy milk
3–4 tbsp cream
1 bunch watercress
½ oz (15 g) butter
parsley, chopped
croutons, butter-fried

Melt 1 oz (25 g) butter in a
large saucepan, add chopped
onion and cook till soft and
translucent, without browning. Add
potato, cucumber and salt and
pepper. Add chicken stock and cook
for 30–40 minutes until vegetables
are soft and tender. Liquidize. Put
puréed soup back into the rinsed
saucepan with the milk. Bring to the
boil, stirring, add the cream and
leave soup to cool. Check watercress
for hard stalks and discard any
discoloured leaves, then sweat in
½ oz (15 g) butter and, when tender,
chop finely and stir into the cooling
soup. Chill and serve with chopped
parsley and a basket of butter-fried
croutons on the table.

POTAGE LORRAIN

(SERVES 4)

A good lunchtime soup from my
super butcher Paul Jeanroy. Since he
retired, Liphook is no longer the
same.

4 oz (110 g) butter
1 medium onion, chopped
2 medium leeks, cleaned and chopped
8 oz (225 g) streaky bacon, sliced thick and cubed
1 lb (450 g) potatoes, cut into 2 in (5 cm) cubes
2½ pt (1.4 l) cold water
salt and pepper
4 small slices wholemeal bread
knob butter

Melt butter in a large pan. Add
onion, leeks and bacon, cook gently
until golden. Add potatoes, water
and season to taste. Leave to simmer
until potatoes are soft (about 20
minutes). Toast the bread. Stir the
soup and check seasoning. Place the
toast in the bottom of a tureen or
serving bowl and pour soup over the
top, stir in a good knob of butter and
serve immediately.

TOMATO AND MINT SOUP

(SERVES 6)

This lovely soup came from David
and Hilary Brown at La Potinière
restaurant in Gullane, Scotland. We
stayed locally for the 1987 Open Golf
Championship and spent a
marvellous evening with the Browns.
We found out afterwards that the
restaurant is famed locally and
booked up for three months ahead,
not surprising with the excellence of
their menus concentrating on fresh
local produce.

8 oz (200 g) onions
2 oz (50 g) butter
2 lb (900 g) ripe tomatoes – leave whole, unskinned and do not remove the stalks
½ pt (75 ml) dry sherry
1 level tbsp caster sugar
1½ tbsp dried mint
salt
fresh mint and cream for serving

Peel the onions and slice finely. Place in a saucepan and cook gently in the butter. Once the onions are softened (do not let them brown) add tomatoes, sherry, sugar and dried mint. Stir with a wooden spoon, cover pan with a lid and cook gently for 40 minutes. Liquidize the soup then pour it through a mouli (or fine sieve) into the rinsed-out pan. The mouli will remove the pips, stalks and skins. Add salt to taste and enough water to give the correct consistency – it should be smooth with plenty of body – don't thin it too much. Reheat and serve with a good teaspoon of whipped cream floating on top of each bowl plus a leaf of fresh mint.

CREAM OF SEAFOOD SOUP

(SERVES 6)

This soup from the Links Hotel at Liphook in Hampshire is one of my personal favourites. The 'Crab and Lobster', as the locals call this hotel, excels with its fresh seafoods and the fattest, freshest crab sandwiches ever seen! It is very important to make the stock with the shells for the unique and delicious flavour. It is not the same made with stock cubes.

8 oz (225 g) butter
3 oz (75 g) flour
½ tsp paprika
2 pt (1.1 l) fish stock made with lobster or crab shells and the claws
1 bay leaf
pinch of marjoram, parsley, salt and pepper
½ tsp ground ginger
1 cup medium dry white wine
4 oz (110 g) brown crab meat
lemon juice
4–6 tsp single cream
fresh parsley, chopped

Make a roux, with butter, flour and paprika. Lightly cook and then add fish stock and whisk slowly, adding the rest of the ingredients. Simmer for 10 minutes. Top each portion with 1 tsp cream and sprinkle with parsley.

CORN CHOWDER

(SERVES 8)

A very quick soup, given to me by my great friend here in Churt, Pauline. She makes it for Saturday lunchtime when all our kids are in and out of her house and mine!

½ onion, chopped
1 oz (25 g) butter
1¼ lb (550 g) frozen sweetcorn, defrosted and salted to taste
6 cups chicken broth, or 1 large tin chicken soup
white pepper
¼ pt (150 ml) cream
parsley, chopped

Sauté onion in butter until soft and transparent, add all other ingredients except cream and parsley. Cover and leave to simmer until the corn is tender, stir in the cream and serve piping hot, sprinkled with parsley and eaten with crunchy granary rolls.

BUTTERFLY CROUTONS

Terribly simple and devastatingly effective. Simply take slices of day-old sliced white bread and using a shaped pastry cutter (I use hearts, stars or daisies) cut the shapes out and fry in butter. Keep warm and serve with soups or any savouries. Pile them high in a basket with white doilies and big sprigs of mint or parsley; they look and smell delicious.

STILTON PÂTÉ

(SERVES 8)

Pat Wood's recipe is a marvellous way of using up the remains of the Christmas Stilton. Try serving it with chunks of crispy fennel as well as crunchy hot brown toast.

8 oz (225 g) Stilton
1 lb (450 g) cream cheese
1 tbsp brandy
⅛ pt (75 ml) double cream
black pepper

Pound Stilton in mortar or food processor until smooth, add half the cream cheese, add brandy *slowly*, rest of cream cheese and finally double cream and pepper.
N.B. Take care not to over-work

cream mix if using a processor. Place in tureen or cocotte dishes. If keeping, cover with clarified butter.

MUSHROOM FROMAGE

(SERVES 4)

Another of Peter's favourites as he loves mushrooms. Very easy to do and perfect for a light supper dish and eaten with crisp brown toast.

4 oz (110 g) butter
1 lb (450 g) button mushrooms, peeled
3 tbsp thick cream
4 dsp grated Gruyère cheese

Melt the butter in a heavy-bottomed saucepan. Add mushrooms, cover and cook slowly until ready, shaking frequently. Take off the heat and add cream. Stir and then heat through. Add cheese. Put into gratin dish or dishes. Sprinkle more cheese on top. Brown under grill. Serve at once.

HELEN'S CAVIAR PIE

(SERVES 8–10)

We had this 'pie' at Helen and Terry Wogan's some three years ago and like everyone else were bowled over by its colour and simplicity; it transforms plain smoked salmon.

6 hard-boiled eggs, shelled
2 oz (50 g) butter
freshly milled black pepper
salt
6 oz (175 g) lumpfish caviar
2 tbsp finely chopped chives or spring onions

Put the eggs, butter and black pepper into a blender – blend until smooth. Taste and season well. Spread this into a 9½ in (24 cm) springform ring pan lightly oiled and the base covered with a circle of greaseproof paper. Chill well for about three hours. Half an hour before serving spread the caviar evenly over the eggs and sprinkle with 1 tbsp of the chives or onions. Then spread the soured cream in a broad band around the edge leaving the centre circle showing the black lumpfish caviar. Freshly sprinkle with remaining chives or onions and chill. Remove the springform side, leave on base and transfer to serving plate. Cut into wedges and serve with smoked salmon and preferably Irish soda bread.

CRAB MOULD

(SERVES 6–8)

This is one of my American recipes. We ate it on a hot summer evening out on the terrace, the barbecue glowing and bowlfuls of crispy green salad to hand.

1 packet gelatin, unflavoured
½ cup cold water
10½ oz (290 g) tin mushroom soup, condensed
1 cup mayonnaise
2 x 3 oz (75 g) packets cream cheese
1 tbsp Worcestershire sauce
1 tbsp onion juice
2 tbsp chopped celery
juice from ½ lemon
2 x 6 oz (175 g) tins crab meat, cheapest

Sprinkle gelatin into cold water. Leave for 2 minutes and then heat gently to dissolve. Heat soup to boil. Add gelatin then cool till thick, stirring frequently to prevent a skin forming. Add everything else except crab. Use mixer to blend. Add crab and place in 1½ pt (850 ml) ring mould. Put into fridge to set. When ready to use, run hot tap gently over outside of mould to loosen contents. Put plate over the top and turn over quickly. Fill the centre with lots of watercress or fresh garden herbs.

SEAFOOD CRÊPES

(SERVES 6–8, OR 4 AS MAIN COURSE)

Another of the recipes I brought back from the United States. I still use this one often; it makes an equally good starter or main course and is delicious.

Batter
4 oz (110 g) flour
pinch of salt
1 egg
1 egg yolk
½ pt (275 ml) milk
1 tbsp melted butter for cooking

Sift the flour and salt into a bowl. Make a well in the centre of the bowl and add the egg and egg yolk and ⅓ of the milk. Stir and blend. When thick and creamy slowly add the rest of the milk, drawing in the flour from the sides. Beat well and leave to stand for 30 minutes. Make pancakes in usual way in a 6 in (15 cm) frying pan and stack one on top of other ready for use. Allow two pancakes per person for a main course, one as a starter.

Filling

6 tbsp butter

6 tbsp flour

1½ medium sized tins lobster soup

4 fl oz (110 ml) stock

6 fl oz (170 ml) cream

2 tbsp Cognac

salt, pepper

1¼ lb (550 g) fresh lobster or crab meat – or 2 large cans of lobster/crab meat

1½ tbsp fresh dill, finely chopped

cheese, for grating over

Melt butter and add flour – stir until smooth and then add lobster soup and stock a little at a time, stirring constantly until smooth. Add cream. Add Cognac, salt and pepper and simmer. Do not boil. Add lobster or crab and dill. Put a little of the filling into each crêpe, roll up and place in buttered dishes. Grate a little cheese over the top and put into oven until nicely brown. Decorate with lots of parsley and if you have them a whole king prawn.

MOTHER'S CHICKEN LIVER PÂTÉ

(SERVES 6)

I make ours exactly as described below – but in bulk. I buy 6 lb (2.7 kg) of liver at a time and I freeze the rest. It freezes beautifully for several months. You can add brandy or other flavourings – but we like ours as it is, creamy, smooth and delicious.

7 oz (200 g) butter

1 small clove garlic

1 medium onion, peeled and finely chopped

12 oz (350 g) chicken livers (buy 1 lb (450 g) and trim)

pinch mixed herbs

½ tsp salt

freshly milled black pepper

Melt 1 oz (25 g) of the butter, put garlic through press and add to butter with onion, fry until pale and translucent. Trim and slice livers, add to hot butter with herbs and seasoning. Cover and cook gently for 5–7 minutes, stirring occasionally. Draw pan off heat and liquidize contents (or put in blender). Cream 5 oz (150 g) of the remaining butter and gradually beat in liver mixture. Spoon into dish, melt remaining 1 oz (25 g) butter and pour over the pâté.

SPINACH ROULADE

(SERVES 8)

This is from my great friend Lynn, and often eaten at her home in Yorkshire. She's a great one, too, for Fillet of Beef en Croûte which she decorates as a cottage with doors, windows and a chimney; it looks amazingly good.

1 lb (450g) spinach, fresh and young leaves

4 eggs, separated

½ oz (15 g) butter

salt and pepper

8 oz (225 g) cream cheese

soured cream

4 oz (110 g) prawns, chopped

tomato sauce

Cook the spinach till tender, drain well. Pass through sieve or put into Magimix (the purée must not become liquid or wet). Stir in the egg yolks one at a time, then add the butter and seasonings. Whisk the whites till firm, then fold into spinach mixture. Have ready a previously prepared swiss roll tin. Use silicone or greaseproof paper to line your tin and lightly butter up the sides to 2 in (5 cm). Spread the mixture and bake in a hot oven at 400 F (200 C) Reg 6 until firm to touch and well risen. Turn out into rack and cover with a damp cloth to stop it hardening. Cool for 2–3 minutes and roll up with a mixture of cream cheese mixed with soured cream and chopped prawns. Serve immediately with hot tomato sauce (see next recipe).

TOMATO SAUCE

(MAKES 1 PT (575 ML))

This is excellent for several dishes, and it also freezes well.

4 oz (110 g) onion, well chopped

2 cloves garlic, crushed

1 oz (25 g) celery and carrots,
    well chopped

1 tbsp olive oil

2 x 28 oz (800 g) tins Italian
    plum tomatoes in their juice

3 tbsp dry white wine

2 tbsp granulated sugar

1 bay leaf

pinch of thyme and a few parsley stalks

salt and pepper

Sweat onion, garlic, celery and carrots in oil over low heat in covered pan until soft, not coloured. Add remaining ingredients. Break up tomatoes with wooden spoon, stir well; bring to boil and simmer briskly uncovered for 15–20 minutes stirring occasionally till sauce is reduced to an interesting but not too thick consistency. Let it cool a little, liquidize and put through coarse sieve and get rid of seeds and débris. Check seasoning.

CRAB MOUSSE

(SERVES 6)

This can be made using salmon instead of the crab.

1 lb (450 g) crab meat

6 oz (175 g) fresh cream cheese

¼ pt (150 ml) mayonnaise

salt and pepper

cucumber slices, fresh prawns and
    twists of lemon for decoration

Aspic

¼ pt (150 ml) cold water

½ oz (15 g) gelatin

1 tbsp lemon juice

1 tbsp wine vinegar

Mix together crab meat. Mix cream cheese and mayonnaise in a liquidizer. Stir in crab meat. Put the water and gelatin in a pan and leave to soak for a few minutes. Then dissolve over a low heat. Take the pan off the heat and add the lemon juice and wine vinegar. Stir in the crab mixture. Season with salt and pepper to taste. Pour into a lightly oiled fish mould or small dishes. Once the mousse has set turn it out onto a serving dish. To do this easily, run the outside of the mould under the hot tap until the contents loosen. Decorate with thin slices of cucumber and fresh prawns with twists of lemon. Serve with brown bread and butter or hot crusty brown bread.

TARRAGON PEARS

(SERVES 8)

Lovely memories of the Spice Box restaurant at Boston Spa flood back every time I make this starter. It was, and is, one of my favourites as I love tarragon in any form.

4 ripe Conference pears,   peeled, halved and cored
fresh mint, finely chopped
walnut halves
Dressing
1 egg
2 oz (50 g) caster sugar
3 tbsp tarragon vinegar
salt and pepper
½ pt (275 ml) double cream
salt and freshly ground   black pepper as required

Place the pears curved side upwards or on a bed of crispy lettuce and coat with the dressing. To make this, break egg into a basin and whisk with a fork. Add sugar and gradually the vinegar. Stand bowl in saucepan over boiling water and stir until it thickens. Take off heat and continue stirring until a thick cream consistency. Leave till cold. Partially whip the cream, fold in to mixture and, when smooth, check the seasoning. Then coat the pears. Chill

until ready to serve, then sprinkle with very finely chopped fresh mint. Decorate the sides of the plate with walnut halves.

BAKED EGGS EN SOUFFLÉ

(SERVES 4)

This recipe came from Penny Smith – I find it just a little bland and often sprinkle finely grated gruyère cheese on top instead of Parmesan.

4 eggs, large
4 tbsp single cream
4 tsp Parmesan cheese, freshly grated
salt and pepper

Separate the eggs, taking care to keep each yolk whole. Place each yoke in a separate small buttered dish, which prevents the yolk from sticking to the side of the dish so that it can easily be placed on top of the soufflé later. Whisk the whites to stiff peaks and quickly fill 4 small ramekins with them. Hollow out the centre of each soufflé and gently place an egg yolk in each hollow. Season lightly with salt and pepper. Pour over a little cream, and sprinkle with Parmesan cheese. Bake in the oven at 400 F (200 C) Reg 6 for 4 minutes or until well risen. N.B. Ensure that the hollow is deep enough to take the yolk, otherwise as the soufflé rises the yolk will fall off.

INSALATA DEI FUNGHI

(SERVES 4–6)

I cannot remember where I got this recipe but I use it frequently for dinner parties and it is always a success. The original recipe called for olive oil but I prefer the lighter taste of sunflower oil.

8 oz (225 g) button mushrooms, finely sliced
olive oil or sunflower oil
1 lemon
2 cloves garlic, finely crushed
Tabasco sauce, 6 shakes
1 tsp caster sugar
salt and black pepper
5 oz (150 g) shrimps
¼ pt (150 ml) double cream
parsley, chopped

Place the mushrooms in an oval serving dish and saturate with olive oil. Stir in the lemon juice, garlic, Tabasco, caster sugar, salt and black pepper. Chill for 1 hour. Stir in the shrimps and double cream. Sprinkle generously with chopped parsley. To serve as a main course, add flaked crab or lobster and serve with crunchy brown rolls.

MUSHROOMS CRÈME FRAÎCHE

(SERVES 6)

We at home all love mushrooms and I do them lots of ways, deep fried, stuffed, grilled with tarragon mustard and often like this as a starter. Crème fraîche is available at most large supermarkets or good delicatessens.

3 tbsp brandy
3 tbsp olive oil or sunflower oil
¼ pt (150 ml) white wine
1 tsp salt
1 medium onion, finely chopped
4 oz (110 g) tin button mushrooms, trimmed
Dressing
¼ pt (150 ml) crème fraîche or whipped/clotted cream
½ tsp French mustard
chopped chives

Put all the ingredients except mushrooms into a pan and simmer for 5 minutes. Add the mushrooms and cover. Simmer for 10 minutes. Cool in liquid, in a basin in the fridge for 12–24 hours. To serve, drain and arrange, per person, on a bed of crispy shredded lettuce. I try to find the unusual and mix red-tipped lettuce, curly endive and endive. Mix the cream and mustard and spoon over the mushrooms. Sprinkle with lots of freshly chopped chives.

HUNTINGDON STUFFED PEARS

(SERVES 4)

This is a variation on Tarragon Pears. I got the recipe from *English Provincial Cooking* – a super book. Make sure the cheese is firm but not hard.

4 oz (110 g) Stilton
1 oz (25 g) butter, fairly soft
1 tbsp double cream
black pepper, freshly milled
1 oz (25 g) walnuts, finely chopped, plus 4 half-kernels
2 large and ripe Conference pears
4 crispy lettuce leaves
juice from ½ lemon

Use a blender, or a bowl and a wooden spoon, to blend together the cheese, butter, cream and black pepper. Mix in the chopped walnuts. Set aside, but do not chill. Peel, halve and core the pears, hollowing out the centres to hold the Stilton mixture (about 2 tsp each). Place on serving plates on a lettuce leaf and brush over the uncovered parts of the pears with lemon juice to prevent browning. Top with a half-walnut and serve within half an hour.

CULLEN SKINK SOUP

(SERVES 6–8)

This soup should be creamy, thick and with a slight bite to it. It is a good soup on a cold day served with chunks of crusty brown bread or oatcakes. 'Ideal for golfers on a cold, windy day,' says Greta Anderson, manageress of the Golf View Hotel at Nairn in Scotland.

4 medium potatoes
1 large onion, finely chopped
2 fillets smoked haddock
1 pt (575 ml) milk
¼ pt (150 ml) cream
salt and pepper

Peel and dice the potatoes, parboil and drain and add the onion. Cut haddock in ½ in (1 cm) cubes and add to the potato and onion. Add the milk and boil for approximately 10 minutes (either top or oven). Add cream, salt and pepper to taste and serve.

Dips and Sauces

We do not give many big drinks parties, preferring small Sunday pre-lunch get-togethers for anything from 20 to 60 people at a time. I often serve dips with lots of chunky things from crudités to tiny meat balls, prawns or tiny chipolatas firmly skewered onto cocktail sticks. A dip should be soft and well-flavoured, hot or cold, but definitely appetizing! These are some of our favourites plus some of our preferred sauces and a few basic ones.

LOUISE'S ARTICHOKE DIP

This dip comes from Louise Brown, wife of Stewart Brown, an ex-Pan-Am captain who became a long-standing friend of my husband during his playing days. Now they live in Antigua where we see them once a year, and this Antiguan dip is one we always request. The Parmesan must be freshly grated, not the packet variety.

1 can artichoke bottoms
1 cup mayonnaise
1 cup freshly grated Parmesan

Blend in Magimix or blender, place in a casserole in the oven for 30 minutes at 350 F (180 C) Reg 4. Meanwhile, open out and flatten several pitta breads, butter and season with Lawley's seasoned salt. Cut into fingers and bake in oven on flat tray until crispy. Serve the dip piping hot with crispy pitta fingers – it's delicious.

MABLE AMBROSE'S CRACKERS

Mable Ambrose is a marvellous huge happy lady who cooks at one of the houses on the Mill Reef Estate in Antigua. There for drinks one day after golf, I found these super biscuits laid out for the dips. I went into the kitchen and met Mable. After lots of thigh-slapping and laughter this was the recipe she gave me.

She used square saltines by Nabisco, though any small crisp salted biscuit (not Ritz) will do.

Soak the biscuits in iced water for just 30 seconds. Take out with a strainer and remove all water. Lightly butter the base of a flat baking sheet. Put the biscuits in and sprinkle generously with Lawley's seasoned salt. Cook in a hot oven for 10–15 minutes and then lower temperature until crisp and brown – about another 5 minutes.

AVOCADO DIP

2 avocados

¼ pt (150 ml) soured cream

ground black pepper

1 small onion, finely grated

squeeze lemon juice

Scoop out flesh from the avocados and mix with a fork, together with soured cream, black pepper, onion and lemon juice. Serve this with a selection of crudités such as sticks of carrot, celery, zucchini, florets of cauliflower and, for a special occasion, prawns spiked onto a cocktail stick.

AMERICAN CURRY DIP

I seem to have collected lots of dips over the years. Some well-known such as blue cheese, avocado and onion but this one from the States is different.

½ cup soured cream

½ cup unsweetened (Hellmann's) mayonnaise

1 tsp curry powder

1 tsp grated onion

Combine all ingredients and refrigerate until wanted. Serve with strips of carrot, zucchini, celery, cucumber, cauliflower, and any other raw vegetables.

FRIED COCONUT

This came from Tobago, and is delicious to nibble with drinks. Very simple, it's made from fresh coconut cut into strips, sprinkled with salt and put into the oven to go crisp. Eat warm or cold.

CREAM CHEESE AND PRAWN DIP

This is particularly good served with crackers and sticks of celery.

8 oz (225 g) cream cheese

½ pt (275 ml) soured cream

1 clove garlic, crushed

¼ tsp hot pepper or Tabasco sauce

salt

2 oz (50 g) prawns, chopped

Cream the cheese until soft and combine with soured cream. Add rest of ingredients and chill well.

CURRY MAYONNAISE

This is super with chicken salads, also the lovely fresh fruit platter one has so often in the United States, and it's equally good with fish. Mix together the following ingredients:

¼ pt (150 ml) mayonnaise

½ tsp ginger

½–1 tsp curry powder

1 pressed clove garlic

1 tsp honey

1 tbsp lime or lemon juice

CAVIAR SAUCE

This we use either as a dip or it is equally delicious in hot jacket potatoes in the winter months.

4 oz (110 g) soured cream

1 tsp onion, finely grated

2 oz (50 g) lumpfish caviar

Combine the soured cream with the onion and add the lumpfish caviar.

SAUCE VERTE

An Alliss favourite. I serve it with all fish and shellfish dishes; it's super with salmon or salmon trout, or with salmon mousse. I can't help thinking that all that green watercress, filled with iron, is doing us the world of good!

½ pt (275 ml) well flavoured mayonnaise
1 tbsp watercress, finely chopped
1 tbsp parsley, finely chopped
1 tbsp tarragon, finely chopped
lemon juice
salt and black pepper

Blend the mayonnaise and all herbs for a few seconds in a blender. Then add lemon juice and seasoning to taste. Chill before serving.

MORNAY SAUCE

½ pt (275 ml) Béchamel sauce
2 oz (50 g) Gruyère or Cheddar cheese, grated
paprika pepper
salt and pepper

Make the basic Béchamel sauce and when it has thickened stir in the cheese and seasonings.

VELOUTÉ SAUCE

¾ oz (20 g) butter
2 tbsp flour
¾ pt (400 ml) chicken stock
3 tbsp single cream
a few drops of lemon juice
salt and pepper

Melt butter, add the flour and cook gently for 1 minute. Stir in the stock and slowly bring to the boil stirring all the time. It should reduce slightly and have a syrupy texture. Take off the heat and add the lemon juice and cream. Check the seasoning. Use with poultry, veal or fish.

BÉCHAMEL SAUCE

1 bay leaf
1 small onion, skinned and sliced
4 peppercorns
½ pt (275 ml) milk
1 oz (25 g) butter
3 tbsp flour
salt and pepper

Put bay leaf, onion and peppercorns with milk into a saucepan and cook gently until boiling. Remove and strain. Melt butter, stir in flour and cook for a minute or two stirring all the time. Carefully add in the strained milk, stirring to make a smooth, lump-free sauce. Simmer for 2–3 minutes. Check for seasoning.

MAYONNAISE

1 egg yolk
pinch of salt and pepper
pinch of dry mustard
¼ pt (150 ml) olive or sunflower oil
1 dsp white wine vinegar
1 dsp warm water

Mix together egg yolk, salt, pepper and dry mustard. Gradually beat in, drop by drop, the olive or sunflower oil. Stop adding oil when mixture is thick and creamy. Beat in white wine vinegar and lastly add warm water.

Main Courses

Main courses should be fun, not too large and should complement your starter. Take care not to put two bland flavours together or equally two strong, spicy courses. A rich main course should preferably be followed by a fruity or clear lemony dessert such as a syllabub. I serve my cheese in the French way, before the dessert and unless it's a very special night I usually only serve two courses plus cheese and a pud.

LEMON CHICKEN

(SERVES 6)

This is a very easy recipe. My husband would eat chicken every day, so I'm always trying different ways. This is a favourite, gleaned originally from my Aunt Jean whose kitchen in Bearley, Warwickshire was a great place of learning for me.

3½ lb (1.6 kg) chicken
2½ oz (65 g) butter
rind of 1 large lemon, grated
rest of lemon, roughly chopped
1 clove garlic, bruised
little cream

Stand the chicken up, slit the skin along the breast bone and round the top of the legs with a very sharp knife. Loosen the skin with your fingers, easing it back to expose the flesh. Soften the butter and mix with the grated lemon rind. Draw back the skin gently and stuff the lemony butter between the flesh and the skin. Put the rest of the lemon inside the chicken with the garlic and roast in the usual way. When ready to serve add the lemony pan juices to the giblet gravy and finish with a little cream. We eat this dish with lots of buttery noodles and a crispy green salad.

SWEETBREADS WITH SPINACH IN CREAM SAUCE

(SERVES 6)

Sweetbreads are a favourite of mine, cooked in any way but preferably in a cream sauce. This recipe is lovely.

1 carrot, peeled and sliced
1 onion, peeled and sliced
1½ pt (850 ml) water
1 bay leaf
salt and pepper
nutmeg
1 tbsp tarragon vinegar
2 lb (900 g) sweetbreads
3 lb (1.4 kg) fresh spinach (or 2 lb/900 g frozen)
2½ oz (65 g) butter
2 shallots, peeled and finely chopped
½ pt (275 ml) double cream
2 medium-sized egg yolks
1 tbsp flour

Add the carrot and onion to the water in a large pan, add the bay leaf, salt, pepper and nutmeg and place over medium heat. Add the vinegar and, when boiling, lower the heat and reduce the liquid to about half. Add sweetbreads and sufficient boiling water, if necessary, to cover them. Bring back to the boil over a low heat and simmer for 20 minutes. Drain and hold under running cold water in a colander. Then remove all skin and membrane from the sweetbreads and set aside. Melt two-thirds of the butter in a heavy iron pan and, when foaming, add shallots and cook on a low heat until they start to colour. Add the sweetbreads cut into slices. Season and cover and leave to braise for 20 minutes or so. Meanwhile wash spinach in several changes of cold water and then cook with just the water clinging to the leaves for about 5 minutes over medium heat. Drain the soft leaves and squeeze dry, keeping the juices. Chop roughly. By this time the sweetbreads should be ready. Lift out with a slotted spoon and put on one side. Add the spinach to the sweetbread juices, season well with salt and pepper and nutmeg. Sprinkle the flour mix well into the juices and add half the cream.

Place the spinach mixture into a shallow ovenproof dish and arrange the sweetbreads on top. Beat the yolks into the remaining cream. Season and pour over the top. Dot the top of the dish with chunks of the remaining butter and cook in a moderate oven at 400 F (200 C) Reg 6 until heated thoroughly and pale golden brown. Do not cook for too long or else the cream will curdle.

Veal Escallops à l'Orange
Turbot à la Champagne

VEAL ESCALLOPS À L'ORANGE

(SERVES 6)

Another very simple dish, particularly useful if you get unexpected guests. I keep escallops in the freezer and I always have lots of oranges so this is a dish I can whip up in about half an hour. It is equally good served with puréed potatoes or buttered noodles.

6 escallops veal
3 oz (75 g) butter
1½ dsp flour
2 large oranges
1½ tbsp brandy
6 fl oz (170 ml) good stock
salt and pepper
parsley, chopped

Sauté escallops in butter until brown. Remove from pan, draw pan off heat and stir in the flour. Grate the rind of 1 orange into the pan, add the strained juice, brandy, stock and seasoning. Bring to the boil, put in the escallops, cover and simmer for 10 minutes. Meanwhile slice and peel and pith the second orange and cut the flesh into rounds, one for each escallop. To serve, put escallops on serving dish, place a round of orange on each and spoon over sauce. Sprinkle with parsley.

VEAL NORMANDY

(SERVES 6)

This always reminds me of my father who loved Calvados, either as an after-dinner liqueur or as a flavouring in food. We took holidays in Normandy and he would regale us with tales from the war, of the villagers' hospitality to the troops, of the hardship and suffering, of the celebrations when the war finally ended.

This is a delicious dish of veal cooked with apples, cream and Calvados, a brandy distilled mainly from apples.

5 oz (150 g) butter
6 escallops or veal fillets (which are delicious)
½ pt (275 ml) double cream
6 tbsp Calvados
2 lb (900 g) dessert apples (Cox's or Golden Delicious)
sugar
salt, black pepper

Melt half the butter and sauté the veal until golden. Place in a shallow ovenproof dish large enough to take them in one layer, cover tightly with foil and put into oven. Deglaze the pan with the cream, scraping the bottom with a wooden spoon, heat slowly until simmering and reduce by about one-third. Add Calvados and mix well, check seasoning, then pour sauce over the meat, re-cover dish tightly and continue cooking for about 30 minutes at 350 F (180 C) Reg 4. Wipe the pan out with kitchen paper, peel core and slice the apples. Melt remaining butter and when foaming add apple slices and cook until golden on both sides. Sprinkle lightly with sugar and glaze, shaking the pan frequently to prevent them sticking; remove and keep warm. To serve; place the apple slices around the sides of the veal on a large serving plate and serve very hot with buttered noodles.

MEDALLIONS OF VEAL WITH LEMON AND TARRAGON

(SERVES 4)

The fillet of veal is, to my mind, the easiest and by far the tastiest way of eating veal. Tender, it takes minutes to sauté for a dinner party and this recipe, collected in Paris at the house of a great friend, Jeannie Decogis, is one I often use and which conjures up magic memories of an evening at the Crazy Horse Saloon.

2 lemons, ripe and juicy
2 oz (50 g) butter
1 lb (450 g) tenderloin of veal, trimmed of fat and sinews and cut into 2 in (5 cm) pieces
salt and freshly ground black peppers
6–8 tbsp dry white wine
1 tbsp tarragon

Pare the rind off one lemon and cut into thin julienne strips. Bring to the boil in cold water, drain and refresh in cold water. Set on one side. Heat 1 oz (25 g) of the butter in a heavy-bottomed frying pan, season the veal and then cook slowly in the hot butter for about 6–7 minutes. Take out the meat with a slotted spoon and keep warm. Pour the wine into the juices, deglaze, scraping up the bits from the bottom of the pan. Reduce down, finally adding the remaining butter, tarragon, seasoning and juice from one lemon. Serve veal covered with the sauce and topped with the lemon julienne strips. I sometimes add cream to the final sauce if I want to make it go further.

PHEASANT À LA JEANROY

(SERVES 8)

I ask my butcher to joint a brace of birds for me into medium pieces as I personally don't like to see a huge piece of bird on my plate. A brace will serve eight easily for a dinner party. Ask the butcher for the bones and make a good stock with a mirepoix of a leek, a carrot and a stick of celery chopped and added to the stock pan.

1 brace pheasants
4 oz (110 g) lardons of green bacon plus a large piece of bacon fat
4 oz (110 g) button mushrooms
pheasant stock
sultanas
Armagnac
2 oz (50 g) butter
1½ oz (40 g) flour

Toss the skinned, jointed and semi-boned pieces in well seasoned flour. Fry in a mixture of half butter, half oil in a heavy-bottomed frying pan. Cook very slowly, turning frequently, until nicely browned. Arrange the pieces in a casserole. Using the same pan, sauté lardons of bacon, about 4 oz (110 g) and about 4 oz (110 g) of halved button mushrooms. Add a little extra butter if needed. Place these on top of the pheasant and cover with a large piece of bacon fat (again ask your butcher). Pour over, to just cover, stock made from the bones and cook in a medium oven for 45 minutes until meat is tender and sauce reduced. Meanwhile soak a handful of plump sultanas in Armagnac and set aside. Make a beurre manié with about 2 oz (50 g) butter and 1½ oz (40 g) flour, add liquid from casserole and pour back over pheasant when sauce is nicely thickened. Pour the sultanas, and the brandy in which they are soaking, over the dish just before serving.

CHICKEN SUPRÊMES EN CROÛTE

(SERVES 4)

I always keep chicken suprêmes in my deep-freeze in case of unexpected visitors. This recipe, with its stuffing, is delicious and you can ring the changes by filling the suprême with pâté, or a mixture of onion and mushroom. Even cheese mixed with chopped ham and celery tastes good.

Stuffing
4 oz (110 g) dried prunes
4 oz (110 g) cooking apples, peeled, cored and chopped
2 small onions, finely chopped
1 oz (25 g) breadcrumbs
little lemon rind
salt and pepper
beaten egg to bind
* * *
4 chicken breasts
4 knobs butter
1 packet frozen puff pastry

Make the stuffing by combining all the ingredients and binding with some of the beaten egg. Make a pocket in each chicken breast and fill with stuffing and a knob of butter. Cut pastry into 4 squares, roll each into a rectangle large enough to wrap around each chicken piece, seal carefully and brush with rest of beaten egg. (I cut out hearts or stars with pastry cutters and cover the tops with these.) Bake on a baking sheet at 400 F (200 C) Reg 6 for about 30–40 minutes. If the pastry browns too quickly, pop a sheet of foil loosely over the top.

STEAK À LA MOUTARDE

(SERVES 4)

Many years ago Peter and I were in Alicante, Spain, on a business trip. Out to lunch in a tiny restaurant, we were served small, thick, butter-tender steaks with a marvellous topping of thick mustard, liberally sprinkled with brown sugar and then popped under the grill until melted and crystallized. It was superb and I've experimented ever since. This is a slightly easier dish to get right. I found, on an earlier version, that I kept overcooking the steak!

4 thick fillet steaks
2 cloves garlic, salt and black pepper
2–3 oz (50–75 g) butter
4 tbsp dry white wine
2 tbsp brandy
2 tsp Dijon mustard
¼ pt (150 ml) double cream
1 dsp parsley, chopped

Rub steaks well with cut garlic and season with a very little salt and black milled pepper. Fry in the hot butter

until sufficiently done. Put on one side and keep hot. Pour the wine into pan and scrape all the lovely juicy bits with a wooden spoon, then add the brandy, the mustard and stir in well. Add the cream and parsley and blend until hot (do *not* boil). Pour sauce over steaks and serve at once.

LONGE d'AGNEAU PERSILLÉE

(SERVES 4–6)

Another from Penny Smith. We love lamb in our household, preferring it well-cooked but moist, with lots of crispy ends for Dad. The mustard gives it a most unusual flavour.

1 boned loin of lamb, well trimmed
1 oz (25 g) dripping
salt and pepper
3 tbsp Dijon mustard
½ oz (10 g) flour
½ pt (275 ml) stock
Stuffing
1 large garlic clove, finely chopped
6 tbsp parsley, chopped
6 oz (175 g) breadcrumbs, salt and pepper

Make sure that the meat is well trimmed of fat and that the gristle that runs along under the eye of the meat has been removed. Ensure that the outer skin or bark has been removed and that there is sufficient fat to protect the outside of the meat during roasting. Mix the stuffing ingredients together and spread over the inside of the meat. Roll it up and tie securely. Spread with dripping, season and place in roasting tin. Put into hot oven (450 F/230 C/Reg 8) for 10 minutes to seal the meat. Reduce oven to 400 F (200 C) Reg 6 and cook for 20 minutes per 1 lb (450 g) plus 20 minutes over. Twenty minutes before end of cooking time, spread the mustard over the meat and cover with some of the stuffing mixture. Return it to the oven to brown. Strain off most of the fat from the pan, add flour to the juices and cook for a few minutes. Add the stock and stir until thickened. Season to taste with salt and pepper.

STUFFED FILLET OF PORK

(SERVES 4)

This is Sarah Wooldridge's recipe. She and her husband, Ian of the *Daily Mail*, have a busy life and food has to be quick, simple and easy to prepare.

1 cooking apple
sugar
butter
1 packet of thyme and parsley stuffing
2 pork fillets
salt and pepper
1 packet of thin streaky rindless bacon

Cut up the cooking apple and soften in a little water, sugar and butter. Prepare the stuffing as per instructions on packet and then add the apple. Slit the fillets lengthways and flatten out (do not cut them completely in half). Season with salt and pepper and put half the stuffing in each fillet all the way along. Close up the fillets (they will stick together

quite well) and wrap them with several rashers of bacon so they are completely covered. Tie up with cooking string if you wish. Put in a buttered oven dish and cook at 350 F (180 C) Reg 4 for 1½ hours. Turn fillets over at halfway stage so they are browned on both sides. Serve in 1 in (2.5 cm) slices with creamed potatoes, cauliflower cheese and a green salad.

HARE PIE

This is the recipe taken from *Gunter's Confectioner's Oracle* of 1830, courtesy of Alan Payne. I must confess to not having tried it yet, but it *is* different!

Parboil a skinned, washed Hare; wash it again; stew it with parsley, sweet marjoram, cloves, lemon juice, allspice, cinnamon, a little nutmeg, thyme, Port wine, savory, eschalots; cover it with veal broth; fill the bottom of a pie dish with rich stuffing and pour in the contents of the stewpan, adding essence of cedratys* and seasoning; cover with raising paste.

* citrus fruit/lemon

RAGOÛT OF HAM

(SERVES 4)

This recipe is a favourite with Peter when my gammon is already boiled and cold in the pantry. Whole green gammons I find enormously good value, feeding many and having something to cut at for sandwiches at lunchtime when I never know how many I'm going to feed!

8 slices cooked gammon, boiled and cooled
1 oz (25 g) butter
1 oz (25 g) flour
¼ pt (150 ml) red wine
1 tsp caster sugar
½ tsp ground cinnamon
black pepper
juice of 1 large orange
rind of this orange, finely grated

Carve 8 thickish slices and trim off all fat and skin. Melt the butter in a large flattish saucepan and turn the slices in the butter over a low heat until warmed through. Put into a fireproof dish, cover with foil and keep hot. Stir the flour into the butter to make a roux and then add the red wine (nothing too heavy). Stir well and then add the caster sugar, ground cinnamon and black pepper. Then add the juice and rind of the orange. The roux should be fairly thick by now, slightly sharp and also sweet. Pour sauce over ham. We eat it with very creamy potatoes and a fresh vegetable.

DUCK BREASTS IN ORANGE

(SERVES 4)

Where would we be without the marvellous chain stores who make it so easy to buy frozen duck breasts? Made with this lovely orangy sauce and served with rice and a crispy green salad, it's easy, delicious and quick to prepare and always gathers compliments!

4 duck breasts
2 oz (50 g) butter
1 pt (275 ml) good stock
juice and zest of 1 large orange, plus 1 small orange cut into slices
salt and pepper
½ oz (15 g) flour
sprigs watercress

Brown the ducks in 1½ oz (40 g) of the butter until golden. Put into a casserole with the stock and seasoning and sprinkle the orange zest over them. Cover and cook at 400 F (200 C) Reg 6 for about 40 minutes or until tender. Transfer to a shallow serving dish and keep hot, leaving the juices in the pan. Melt the remaining butter in a saucepan, blend in the flour and make a sauce by adding the orange juice and reserved gravy. Cook for 2 minutes and pour over ducks. Decorate with orange slices and sprigs of watercress.

CHICKEN WITH PEACHES

(SERVES 4)

This dish I only make in the months when I can get fresh peaches because I find the taste of tinned ones bears no comparison. The original recipe also called for 'poussin', meaning a whole young bird, but I find this too much on a plate so I adapted the recipe to chicken breasts. The original recipe came from a manor house in Surrey - which had peach trees trained on the kitchen walls. I have been persevering ever since with my peach tree – but every year one or other dreaded lergy gets to it and I have to start all over again!

4 peaches, blanched and peeled, cut in half and stoned

2 tsp caster sugar

¼ tsp nutmeg, freshly grated

¼ pt (150 ml) white wine

4 large chicken suprêmes

some seasoned flour

4 slices fresh lemon

4 rashers bacon

4 oz (110 g) butter

4 tbsp double cream

⅓ pt (185 ml) chicken stock

salt and pepper

Put the peaches outside uppermost in a flat fireproof dish, sprinkle with the sugar and nutmeg and pour over the wine. Toss the chicken pieces in seasoned flour, lay a slice of lemon on each breast and cover with a slice of bacon. Put into roasting pan with half the butter. Bake at 400 F (200 C) Reg 6 for 20–30 minutes. Put the peaches in at the bottom of the oven. When chicken is tender, dish up onto a large flat platter. Arrange the peaches around chicken and keep dish hot. Pour off the butter from the roasting pan, stir the cream into the juices left, stir hard, then add stock and the wine juice from the peaches and stir again. Check for seasoning. Pour sauce over the chickens. When I serve it up I place a tiny, deep blue borage flower in each peach hollow!

CASSEROLE OF VENISON WITH CHERRIES

(SERVES 4–6)

Michael Gill of the Pool Court Hotel, who gave me this recipe, has a reputation for serving delicious food, and this casserole has become a favourite with us. Do make sure the venison is boned by your butcher and is well hung and tender.

Marinade

1 pt (575 ml) chicken stock

10 juniper berries

2 bay leaves

1 onion, peeled and roughly chopped

4 oz (110 g) carrots, peeled, washed and roughly chopped

4 oz (110 g) celery, washed and roughly chopped

2 tbsp corn oil

1 lemon, the zest removed and blanched for garnish

lemon juice for marinade

*   *   *

2 lb (900 g) boned shoulder of venison

3 oz (75 g) unsalted butter

6 shallots, peeled and roughly diced

2 fl oz (60 ml) kirsch

2 tbsp plain flour

6 fl oz (170 ml) red Bordeaux

beurre manié, consisting of 1 oz (25 g) soft butter mixed with 1 oz (25 g) plain flour

10 oz (275 g) black cherries, stoned

salt and pepper

Boil chicken stock and stir in the remainder of the marinade ingredients. Allow to cool. Place venison in the marinade and leave for 10 hours. (Do not leave for any longer

as this will tend to dry the meat).
Drain and brown the meat using a
little unsalted butter in a thick-
bottomed pan with the chopped
shallots. Flame with the kirsch.
When extinguished, add the flour
and cook for 5 minutes. Add the red
wine and the strained marinade.
Simmer for about 2 hours or until
tender. If the sauce is not the correct
consistency, thicken with beurre
manié. Add cherries 10 minutes
before serving and check for
seasoning. To serve, carve thick slices
off the joint and place on hot plates.
Surround with cherries and offer the
sauce separately. Sprinkle the meat
with zested lemon for garnish and
colour.

CALVES' LIVER
IN CITRUS SAUCE

(SERVES 4)

Another of Michael Gill's 'specials'
and special for us because we both
love liver. When you buy your calves'
liver ask your butcher to slice it very
thinly.

4 oranges
1 tbsp caster sugar
1 lime
2 lemons
2 oz (50 g) plumped raisins
3 fl oz (85 ml) orange curaçao
3 fl oz (85 ml) brandy
1 lb (450 g) calves' liver, thinly sliced
watercress to decorate

Thinly peel the skin from three of the
oranges and cut into strips. Place in a
little water with the caster sugar.

Bring to the boil and then allow to
cool. Segment the three oranges
taking care to get no pith and squeeze
the juice from the fourth. Peel and
segment the lime and the lemons.
Any remaining juice should be added
to the squeezed oranges. Cover the
raisins with the curaçao and brandy.
Bring to the boil and then leave to
cool. Season the liver lightly and then
pan-fry in butter. Cook very lightly
leaving it slightly pink in the centre.
Divide between the four plates and
make an attractive arrangement of
the orange, lemon and lime segments.
Sprinkle the orange zest and raisins
on top. To finish the sauce, pour the
liquor from the raisins into the pan,
boil to reduce by half, pour on the
orange and lime juices, reduce by half
again, add the veal stock and further
reduce until a syrupy consistency is
reached. All this should be done over
a high heat. Check for seasoning and
then strain the sauce over the liver. It
should be re-heated quickly under
the grill for a few seconds before
serving. Decorate with lots of fresh
watercress.

SAUTÉED KIDNEYS
IN BRANDY
AND ORANGE SAUCE

(SERVES 6)

Not a dish I serve often for guests as I
find many people are not fond of
kidneys. I tend to cook this for
ourselves and close friends.

12 lambs' kidneys
2 oz (50 g) butter
olive oil

3 tbsp plain flour, well seasoned with
    black pepper and a little salt

2 large onions, chopped

1 dsp oregano or rosemary

juice of ½ lemon

juice of 1 orange

2 tbsp brandy

4–5 fl oz (110–150 ml) single cream

parsley, well chopped

Skin and slice the kidneys, removing core. Melt butter and oil together in a large heavy-based pan. Dip kidneys into seasoned flour, fry gently for 3–5 minutes. Add the onions, cover and sweat together with kidneys. Stir in herbs and lemon and orange juice. Simmer for 10 minutes. Stir in brandy. Mix well, then swirl in cream. Sprinkle with lots of parsley.

FILLETS OF SOLE
À LA CHANTAL

(SERVES 4)

This is another of my French butcher's recipes. Deceptively simple, it is always a success and takes only 40 minutes to prepare. From the Ile de France area which contains many of the choicest alimentary products of France. Chantal, by the way, is the name of his daughter.

12 fillets of sole (or plaice),
    skinned and de-boned

salt and pepper

3–4 oz (75–110 g) butter

2 tbsp whisky

1 tbsp double cream

4 oz (110 g) grated cheese
    (I use Emmental)

Preheat oven to 350 C (180 F) Reg 4. Arrange the fillets in a buttered flameproof dish with three-quarters of the butter. Cook, uncovered, in the oven for about 10 minutes. Take the dish and place it over a hot flame, then flame the dish with the whisky – not as complicated as it sounds, just tip the whisky on one side and ignite it. Pour over the cream, add the grated cheese and remaining butter and put back in the oven until golden brown – some 15 minutes. Serve with buttered boiled potatoes.

BAKED TROUT
WITH CREAM

(SERVES 4)

We have a marvellous trout farm very near to us, indeed they seem to have popped up all over the countryside. Baked Trout with Cream is what I do when I want a variation on Trout with Almonds.

4 fresh trout (should be bright-eyed
    and have glossy scales)

butter

2 tbsp shallots, finely chopped

¼ pt (150 ml) dry white wine

juice of 1 lemon

2 tbsp parsley, finely chopped

1 tbsp dill or tarragon, finely chopped

salt

freshly ground black pepper

¼ pt (150 ml) double cream

2 tbsp breadcrumbs, finely grated

assortment of fresh herbs

lemon quarters

Clean the trout. Butter a shallow fireproof baking dish generously and sprinkle with the shallots. Arrange the fish on top, side by side. Add the wine and strained lemon juice and sprinkle with the parsley and dill or tarragon. Season to taste with salt and black pepper. Bring the dish to the boil on top of the cooker and then transfer to a moderate oven (375 F/ 190 C/Reg 5) and bake for about 15 minutes. Heat the cream to blood heat, pour over trout, sprinkle with the breadcrumbs and return to oven until the crumbs are brown and crispy. A few sprigs of fresh herbs on the serving plate and lots of lemon quarters finishes the dish to perfection.

TURBOT
À LA CHAMPAGNE

(SERVES 4)

A dish from our travels to Brittany, France. For me the meaty texture of turbot is preferable to sole or plaice. Look for fresh-smelling white fish and you will not be disappointed with this recipe. We like it with tiny new Jersey potatoes and decorate the dish with branches of fresh herbs to complement the simplicity of the fish.

4 oz (110 g) butter
2 tbsp olive oil
2 shallots, finely chopped
6 oz (175 g) button mushrooms, thinly sliced
4 turbot fillets, boned and skinned
6 tbsp fish stock, made with the bones
½ bottle champagne
salt and white pepper
¼ pt (150 ml) double cream
1 tbsp cornflour

Put half the butter in a large frying pan with the oil and sauté the shallots until transparent, add the mushrooms and continue cooking until tender. Take them out with a slotted spoon and put on one side. Add the remaining butter and sauté the fish until just lightly coloured, adding the mushroom mixture, the fish stock and half the champagne to just barely cover the fish. Season to taste, simmer very slowly, with the pan covered with foil, for a few more minutes until the fish is cooked through; take out the fillets, place in the serving dish and keep warm. Add the cream to the liquid, simmer very gently until the cream is warm, then add cornflour (mixed with a little cold water) and cook over a very low heat until sauce is smooth. When ready to serve, add the remaining champagne and simmer gently until sauce is medium-hot again. Pour over turbot and serve immediately.

CÔTELETTE
DE SAUMON
À LA MONTPELLIER

(SERVES 6 AS A FISH COURSE OR
3 AS A MAIN COURSE)

This was the fish course at our Grand Dinner Party, and is well worth the extra effort needed.

3 x 6 oz (175 g) salmon steaks middle cut)
½ head radicchio
2 sprigs parsley
3 eggs
1 lemon

truffles or truffle paste to decorate

Court Bouillon

1 pt (575 ml) white wine

4 sheets gelatin, soaked

1 carrot

½ onion

2 bay leaves

¼ oz (7 g) peppercorns

juice of 2 lemons

Montpellier Butter

8 oz (225 g) butter

1 oz (25 g) chervil

1 oz (25 g) tarragon

1 oz (25 g) spinach

½ clove garlic

½ oz (15 g) dill

To make the court bouillon, add to the white wine the carrot, onion, bay leaves and peppercorns, and bring to the boil. Add the squeezed soaked gelatin and make sure it dissolves. Squeeze the juice of 2 lemons into this. Place the salmon steaks into the court bouillon and poach. The court bouillon should just simmer for about 20–25 minutes or when the centre bone comes away easily. Take off the stove and allow to fully cool, then chill with the salmon still in the court bouillon. Boil and shell the eggs. Make the Montpellier butter by blending all the ingredients together. The butter should be light green in colour. Remove salmon carefully from court bouillon onto a wire tray. Skin and take out bones and lightly clean the surface of the salmon. Cut the salmon steaks in half down the centre. Spread the butter thinly along the surface of the salmon cutlets. Place in fridge to set. Decorate the cutlets with truffles or truffle paste

and glaze with the court bouillon. Place on a flat or plate with a wedge of lemon, picked parsley, shredded radicchio and half-egg pipped with yolk and excess Montpellier butter.

MOULES MARINIÈRE

(SERVES 4)

My favourite mussels recipe – a classic but very simple to prepare.

2 qt (2.2 l) mussels

black pepper

2 shallots, chopped

2 tbsp parsley, chopped

1 tsp thyme

1 glass white wine

4 oz (110 g) butter

1 tbsp double cream

parsley to garnish

Scrape the mussels clean with a small clean nailbrush and wash quickly in several changes of water (do not soak). Put mussels in large pan, season with pepper and add the shallots, parsley, thyme and white wine. Put pan over high heat and cook until the mussels open, shaking the pan vigorously to make sure they all get equal heat. Remove as soon as the mussels are open. Strain the juice into a large saucepan, bring back to the boil and add the butter bit by bit. When the liquid has reduced by about half take off the heat and stir in cream. Remove any half-shells from the mussels and *discard* any that have not opened. Put mussels into heated serving dish, pour over the sauce, sprinkle with parsley and serve immediately with crusty brown bread.

SEAFOOD PIE

(SERVES 6)

Whenever I say 'Fish Pie' for supper there is a groan of protest from my family. Nothing daunted I carry on and make it and, hey presto, come the end of supper, there is not a spoonful left. I think it is the thought of fish pie that puts most people off, but this one is simple to do, economical and very good.

2 lb (900 g) fish (mix haddock and cod plus scallops and prawns if liked)
1–1½ pt (575–850 ml) milk
½ oz (15 g) butter
salt and pepper
generous sprig parsley
3–4 eggs, hardboiled and chopped
Sauce
2 oz (50 g) butter
2 oz (50 g) flour
2 fl oz (60 ml) single cream
salt, black pepper, paprika
Topping
6 oz (175 g) flour
3 oz (85 g) butter
3 oz (85 g) Gruyère and Cheddar, mixed
1 tbsp parsley, finely chopped

Cook the white fish in enough milk to cover, a knob of butter, salt, pepper and parsley. When cooked lift out the fish, cool, skin, bone and flake. Keep the milk for the sauce. For sauce melt the butter, stir in the flour and cook for 1 minute. Slowly add the milk that you have kept stirring constantly until smooth and creamy. Sauce should be thick enough to well coat the back of a spoon. Add cream and seasonings and pour over fish in a prepared pie dish. Add chopped egg and shellfish, if used, and mix well. Make topping by rubbing flour into butter until fine crumbs, add cheese and parsley. Sprinkle on top of pie, dot with butter and bake in a moderate oven for approximately 30 minutes until the top is gorgeously golden and crispy. We eat ours with a salad of sliced tomatoes and avocados and crusty French bread.

HIGHLAND BAKED SALMON AND LEMON BUTTER SAUCE

(SERVES 2)

This is from The Belfry Hotel, the National Professional Golf Centre. I have passed the recipe on as they gave it to me but I must confess that when I cook it I do it in foil and turn it out into a shallow dish to serve.

2 oz (50 g) butter	
2 x 6 oz (175 g) salmon fillet, skinned and boned	
1 oz (25 g) carrot	*cut into fine*
1 oz (25 g) leek	*strips and*
1 oz (25 g) celery	*blanched in*
1 oz (25 g) green pepper	*boiling water*
juice from ½ lime	
2 fl oz (60 ml) white wine	
pinch chopped chives	
seasoning	
parsley	
Sauce	
4 oz (110 g) butter	
2 egg yolks	
2 fl oz (60 ml) malt vinegar	
juice from ½ lemon	
seasoning	

Form envelopes from two rectangles of greaseproof paper measuring 14 in x 10 in (35 cm x 25 cm). Fold in half and round the corners with scissors. Open out to form the envelope in which the contents will be baked

Place half the butter in the middle of the right-hand side half of each envelope. Lay the salmon fillet on top of the butter. Place the fine strips of blanched vegetables on top of both the salmon: pour on top the lime juice and white wine. Sprinkle over the chopped chives and season well. Fold the left-hand side of the greaseproof paper over the filling and seal well. Bake in a moderate oven at 350 F (180 C) Reg 4 for 10–15 minutes. To make the sauce, melt the butter over a bain marie. Whisk together the egg yolks and vinegar and lemon juice over a low heat until the mixture begins to thicken. Slowly whisk in the warm melted butter to form the butter sauce. Check for correct seasoning and adjust if necessary. Add a little hot water to correct the consistency. To serve, put the salmon-filled envelope on a plate lined with a gold doily. Garnish with the ½ lime and crispy parsley. Cut the envelope to receive the full bouquet of the filling. Serve the sauce separately.

CRAB GUMBO

(SERVES 2)

This is a San Diego recipe. I must confess to rarely buying fresh crab as my butcher has beautiful crabmeat already freshly prepared. Preparing fresh crab is a very time-consuming job but one which I thoroughly enjoy when I have time to mess about.

2 lb (900 g) fresh crab

1 whole tomato, diced

½ red pepper, chopped

½ onion, chopped

1 garlic clove, crushed

1 bay leaf

½ tsp paprika and marjoram

4 oz (110 g) peeled prawns

1 glass medium white wine

lemon juice

½ pt (275 ml) Béchamel sauce (see page 95)

salt and pepper

1 tsp mustard

Place the fresh crab into boiling water and let it simmer for 20 minutes. When the crab has cooled down, pick out the meat and place in the cleaned crab shell on a soufflé dish. Fry the diced tomato, pepper and onion together. Then add the garlic, bay leaf, herbs, prawns, wine and lemon juice. Simmer for 2 minutes. Now add all the above to the Béchamel sauce and season with salt and pepper and add the mustard. Simmer for 10 minutes and mask over the crab meat, put under a hot grill until pale brown and bubbling.

SCALLOPS IN NOILLY PRAT SAUCE

(SERVES 4)

A lovely dinner party dish which is not too difficult or time-consuming, specially if you buy your scallops already prepared. This is another Yorkshire recipe from Michael Gill and he serves separate plates of tiny, beautiful crisply cooked vegetables with it.

16 king scallops

16 fl oz (450 ml) Noilly Prat vermouth

shallots, finely chopped

10 fl oz (280 ml) fish stock, made with bay leaves, juniper berries and bouquet garni

½ pt (275 ml) double cream

12 oz (350 g) unsalted butter

lemon juice

salt and pepper, freshly milled

If using fresh scallops, prise open the scallop shells retaining the natural juices for the marinade. Clean and prepare in the usual manner. Cut the scallops in half and marinate for 30–40 minutes in the Noilly Prat, shallots and juices. Stir occasionally. Remove and add the Noilly Prat to the fish stock. Bring to the boil. Add the scallops and poach for 5–6 minutes. Lift out and keep warm. Reduce the stock and Noilly Prat liquid to almost a glaze (this will be dark caramel in colour). Whisk in the cream and bring gently to the boil. Remove from heat and whisk in the butter a little at a time until the sauce is light and airy. If necessary, correct the seasoning with a little lemon juice, salt and pepper, and additional Noilly Prat. Place the scallops on a warm dish and coat with a little sauce, offering the remainder separately.

FRIED FISH WITH PUERTO RICO SAUCE
(Mojo Isleno)
(SERVES 12)

Bruce Forsyth's lovely wife Winnie gave me this recipe, from her native Puerto Rico, and I've eaten it often at their house.

4 lb (1.8 kg) fish slices (try cod or haddock) 1 in (2.5 cm) thick

2 tbsp salt

1 cup olive oil

1 large clove garlic, peeled and crushed

Sauce

½ cup olive oil

2½ lb (1.1 kg) onions, peeled and sliced

1½ cups water

24 olives, stuffed with pimentos

2 tbsp capers

4 oz (110 g) tin pimentos, cut in tiny slices in their juice

2 x 8 oz (225 g) tins tomato sauce

2 tbsp vinegar

1 tbsp salt

2 bay leaves

Prepare sauce by mixing ingredients and cooking over moderate heat for about 1 hour. When sauce is nearly done, season fish with salt and fry as follows. Put oil and garlic into a frying pan. Brown garlic over moderate heat. Remove garlic and place in the pan as many slices of fish as will fit. Brown at moderate heat on both sides. Reduce heat to low and cook for about 15 minutes, or until fish flakes easily when tested with a fork. Fry remaining slices in same way. Cover with the sauce and serve.

DUCK À LA CAROLINE

(SERVES 4)

British Car Auctions at Frimley in Surrey has a super restaurant under the watchful eye of Caroline Harvey. Her dinner parties are superb and her recipe for duck is delicious.

---

1 fresh duck

sea salt

1 wine glass Mandarine
(French liqueur flavoured
with tangerine) or Orange Curaçao

Salad

watercress

oranges, thinly sliced

burnt almond flakes

orange juice

Lea and Perrin sauce

Prick duck all over with a sharp fork and place upside-down on a trivet in a hot oven, and leave for 1 hour. Then, turn over and sprinkle heavily with sea salt; return to oven until cooked and crisp. Remove from oven and allow to relax. Carve the flesh off the carcass into four joints, i.e. 2 breast and 2 thighs and legs. Having strained all the fat from the pan, return the jointed pieces of duck. Pour over one generous wine glass of Mandarine, baste thoroughly and set alight to burn off excess fat and make for impressive presentation when flaming. Serve with salad of watercress and thinly sliced oranges, topped with burnt almond flakes. Dress with a little orange juice and Lea and Perrin sauce.

LANGOUSTINES AU GINGEMBRE

(SERVES 4)

A Turnberry recipe – a bit complicated but with a very unusual flavour and guaranteed to be a dinner party success. Much better with fresh scampi!

---

1 oz (25 g) butter

1 green apple

1 lemon

1 jar stem ginger

salt and pepper

32 pieces fresh scampi (1 pack frozen)

1 pt (575 ml) double cream

1 egg yolk

parsley to garnish

Melt butter in a heavy-bottomed pan. Peel, core and dice the apple and put into a little water with the juice of the lemon. Take two of the whole gingers and dice. Take one whole ginger and cut into fine strips, and wash in a little water. Season the scampi and sauté in the butter, when half cooked remove from pan. Add diced apple (strained) and diced ginger to the butter; and pour some of the ginger syrup into the pan, reduce a little. Add ¾ pt (450 ml) double cream and reduce by half by boiling. Add scampi. Whip up lightly the remaining cream. Remove pan from heat, add beaten egg yolk and whipped cream. Put into serving dish and glaze under a hot grill. (Take care not to boil). Sprinkle the top with ginger strips and parsley.

SAUTÉ OF BEEF STROGANOFF

(SERVES 2)

A classic favourite, something to make for that special supper for 2–4 people. This recipe came from the Turnberry Hotel.

8 oz (225 g) fillet of beef, tail end

2 oz (50 g) butter

salt

pepper

paprika

1 oz (25 g) shallots, finely chopped

4 oz (110 g) sliced mushrooms

1 measure brandy

¼ pt (150 ml) strong beef stock

½ pt (275 ml) cream

2 gherkins cut into fine strips

juice of ¼ lemon

1 oz (25 g) parsley, chopped

Cut the fillet tail into strips ½ in x 2 in (1 cm x 5 cm) thick. Place the butter into the pan over a fierce heat. Add beef strips, season with salt, milled pepper and paprika. Allow to cook rapidly for a few minutes – the strips should be brown but underdone. Drain beef into colander. Pour butter back in pan. Add chopped shallots and sliced mushrooms. Add measure of brandy, flame it. Then add beef stock and reduce till only covering the bottom of the pan. Add the cream. Reduce by a quarter. Add the gherkins and the beef. Add the lemon juice but do not re-boil. Place in a dish and sprinkle with lots of chopped parsley. Serve with braised rice (see next recipe).

BRAISED RICE

(SERVES 2)

1 whole onion, finely chopped

2 oz (50 g) butter

1 bay leaf

1 mug long grain rice

2 mugs chicken stock

salt

pepper

Cook onion in 1 oz (25 g) melted butter. Add bay leaf and rice. Cook gently without colouring for 2–3 minutes. Add the stock to the rice. Season, cover with butter paper and bring to boil. Place in hot oven for 17 minutes exactly. Remove immediately into another dish. Correct the seasoning and add 1 oz (25 g) butter. Serve in an earthenware dish.

SUPRÊME OF CHICKEN LANGOUSTÉ

(SERVES 4)

This is Geoff's recipe from Old Thorns Golf and Country Club. I tried it first on New Year's Eve, 1986 and it was an unqualified success.

4 x 5 oz (150 g) chicken suprêmes

8 spinach leaves (medium)

2 oz (50 g) butter

4 medium prawns

seasoned flour

beaten egg

breadcrumbs

5 oz (150 g) lobster soup

¼ pt (150 ml) double cream

brandy, optional

Suprême of Chicken Langousté

Skin chicken and remove knuckle bone and chicken fillet. Place suprême between two layers of plastic (a plastic freezer bag will be ideal for this). Gently hammer the chicken in between the plastic with a heavy object such as the side of a steak tenderizer or the edge of a rolling pin, until twice its original size. Repeat with all suprêmes. Blanch spinach leaves in boiling salt water for approximately 3 minutes and gently plunge into cold water. Season and brush with melted butter the inside face of the suprêmes and leave flat on the work surface. Cover each suprême with spinach leaves (two each should be ample), leaving one edge clear by about 1 in (2.5 cm). Remove heads from the prawns and make a row of small cuts across the front of each prawn to make it straight. Place the folded prawn on the suprême, opposite the clear edge, and roll the suprême around it. The clear edge will seal itself to the outside of the chicken. Repeat for all four suprêmes. Each suprême now resembles a fat cigar and should be kept in this shape as far as possible. Try using a cocktail stick if they unfold. Pass each through seasoned flour, beaten egg and breadcrumbs (fresh white if possible). Cook by sealing them in a deep fat fryer for about 4 minutes at 375 F (190 C) Reg 5 and finish in a medium oven for about 15 minutes. Heat lobster soup and half the cream together, add a little brandy if desired and season to taste. Place suprêmes on a chopping board and with a sharp knife cut diagonally across each into a small and large half. Put the smaller pieces directly out on the plate for

service and slice the larger ones at about ½ in (1 cm) thick parallel to the cut. These are placed around the uncut piece and the lobster sauce is poured around the chicken. A teaspoon of double cream dropped into the sauce on the plate and pulled with a knife in 6 directions will give you that professional finish.

PORK STEW WITH SAUERKRAUT
(SERVES 4–6)

Sauerkraut always reminds me of my stay in Germany, but this recipe actually came from the Dormy Hotel in Ferndown. John Clark, the head chef, gave me this recipe in memory of my father-in-law, Percy, and his days at Wannsee Golf Club in Germany before the 1939 war.

small joint of pork from the leg
4 oz (110 g) butter
1 carrot, finely diced
1 onion, finely diced
1 leek, finely diced
2 sticks celery, finely diced
pinch mixed herbs
1 bay leaf
1 clove garlic, crushed
1 pt (575 ml) cider
2 pt (1.1 l) brown veal stock
3 oz (75 g) cornflour mixed to a paste with cold water
2 apples, sliced
seasoning

Cut off fat from pork joint and dice the lean. Place the butter into pan, and when beginning to bubble add diced pork, diced vegetables, mixed herbs, bay leaf and garlic. Fry all together until meat is sealed and brown. Take meat out of pan. Add the cider. Reduce by half and add veal stock. Thicken with the cornflour, stirring continuously until thick. Cook for 20 minutes and then add the meat. Bring back to the boil and cook in oven for 2 hours at 375 F (190 C) Reg 5. For the last 15 minutes of cooking, add sliced apples. Correct seasoning, and serve in earthenware dish, sprinkled with parsley.

Serve with sauerkraut (see next recipe).

SAUERKRAUT – PICKLED WHITE CABBAGE

(SERVES 4–6)

1 lb (450 g) sauerkraut
1 whole onion stuck with cloves
2 carrots
6 peppercorns
6 juniper berries
bouquet garni
½ pt (275 ml) white stock

Season sauerkraut. Place in casserole or pan suitable for oven. Add whole onion and carrots, peppercorns, juniper berries and bouquet garni. Barely cover with good white stock. Cover with butter paper and lid. Cook slowly in moderate oven for 3–4 hours. Remove the bouquet garni and onion. Cut carrots into slices. Dress sauerkraut in a vegetable dish and garnish with the slices of carrot.

VEGETABLES

I sometimes think I could become a vegetarian. There is such a choice available from the exotic to the good old English cabbage. Do you remember the school cabbage, all wet and tasteless and very soft – there was always half an inch of water in the bottom of the dish and heaven help you if you were last in line to be served! But cabbage cooked in a minimum of water, or steamed, still crunchy and well seasoned with butter, salt and black pepper, is delicious. And when you think of what is available all the year round – small crisp Kenyan beans, courgettes from Spain, avocados, peppers, aubergines to make ratatouille with. Fennel, that lovely liquorice-tasting bulb that you can do so much with – served hot with cream sauce, rolled in ham and coated with a cheese sauce, casseroled with tomatoes and peppers and mushrooms. And artichokes, in purées, soups, soufflés, the list is endless!

The following are just a few of my favourites, from the exotic to the simple carrot.

PURÉE OF SPINACH

(SERVES 4)

Purées of different vegetables are always a favourite – so easy to do and they look so attractive. I like to serve two different kinds with perhaps a potato lyonnaise and a simple meat like veal escallop.

2 lb (900 g) spinach
4 tbsp Béchamel sauce (see page 95)
nutmeg, freshly grated if possible
salt and pepper
cream
roasted almonds, chopped

Take the young fresh leaves of the spinach and wash well in cold running water to get rid of any grit. Take out the stalks. Cook the spinach in the minimum of water (just as you lift it out of the bowl). Drain very well and put into processor/blender. Add the Béchamel sauce to the spinach and blend until smooth, add nutmeg and seasonings. I swirl a little cream into it just before serving and top with chopped roasted almonds.

PURÉE OF SWEDE

(SERVES 4–6)

1 large tender swede
½ oz (15 g) butter
salt and freshly ground black pepper
cream
sprigs watercress

Peel and chop the swede into large dice and cook in salted water until very soft. Drain well and put into blender. Add the butter, salt and freshly ground black pepper and blend until smooth. Swirl in some cream before serving, with a few sprigs of watercress or finely chopped parsley to finish.

RED CABBAGE BRAISED WITH APPLE

(SERVES 6)

1 small red cabbage, shredded
1 oz (25 g) butter
1 large onion, sliced
1 large cooking apple, peeled and sliced
1 tbsp brown sugar
2 tbsp wine vinegar
2 tbsp water
little kneaded butter

Heat the oven to 350 F (180 C) Reg 4 and lightly butter a small ovenproof casserole dish. Blanch the cabbage in boiling salted water for 2 minutes and drain well. Melt butter in a frying pan over low heat and gently cook the onion and apple until soft. Mix the sugar, vinegar and water together. Put a layer of cabbage in the casserole, season, sprinkle over a little of the sugar and vinegar mixture and then a layer of apple and onion mixture, season again and sprinkle with sugar and vinegar. Continue these layers finishing with a layer of cabbage. Cover with a butter paper and a lid and cook in the centre of the oven for about 1 hour. Mix in the kneaded butter and return for another 5 minutes.

FLAGEOLET WITH CREAM

(SERVES 5–6)

12 oz (350 g) flageolet beans (I buy them frozen)
6 rashers streaky bacon
½ oz (15 g) butter
1 large onion, finely chopped
salt and freshly ground black pepper
2 egg yolks
¼ pt (150 ml) double cream

Cook the beans as directions on packet. Drain and set on one side to keep warm. Cut bacon into small strips, melt the butter and gently fry bacon until the fat runs, do not let it brown. Remove the bacon and put on one side. Add the onion to the bacon fat and again fry until tender but not brown. Return the beans and bacon to the pan and season. Beat the egg yolks and cream in a small bowl, stir into the beans and mix well. Reheat if necessary but take care not to boil or the eggs will curdle. Serve at once.

GLAZED CARROTS

(SERVES 4)

1 lb (450 g) carrots
4 tbsp chicken stock
1 tbsp sugar
salt
4 tbsp butter
parsley

Clean carrots, slice thickly and place in cold water in a small pan. Blanch for 2 minutes and drain. Simmer carrots very slowly with chicken stock, sugar, salt and butter until the carrots have absorbed the liquid without browning and have taken just a little colour. Sprinkle with parsley. You can do exactly the same with tiny white onions; delicious.

PURÉE OF CELERIAC AND POTATOES

(SERVES 4–6)

Celeriac is a very versatile vegetable, try it with carrots in soup or try parboiling thick slices and then roasting them around the joint on Sunday.

1 large celeriac
4 oz (110 g) butter
potatoes to the same weight as the celeriac (or according to personal taste)
salt and pepper
2 tbsp cream
parsley

Peel and dice the celeriac, blanch in boiling water for 10 minutes, drain off the water and add 3 oz (75 g) of the butter to the pan, cover and cook gently for 20 minutes. Put into blender until smooth. Peel and boil the potatoes, when soft mash them well (no lumps, if in doubt put into blender). Add the celeriac to the potato and season. Whisk in remaining butter and cream. Sprinkle with lots of parsley before serving.

PAUL'S RATATOUILLE

(SERVES 4)

Delicious and very quick to make; best when the greenhouse is brimming over with tomatoes.

3–4 tbsp olive oil
4 aubergines, sliced but not peeled
4 courgettes, sliced but not peeled
1 large onion, chopped
1 clove garlic, put through a press and finely chopped
3 sweet red peppers
2–3 large tomatoes, skinned and quartered
salt and black pepper
1 tbsp fresh parsley, chopped

Heat the oil and gently fry the aubergines and courgettes. Add the onion, garlic, peppers and tomatoes and fry thoroughly. Reduce the heat, check the seasoning and simmer briskly uncovered for about 45 minutes so the juices evaporate to ensure a nice thick consistency. Sprinkle with chopped parsley.

HOT SPICED BEETROOT

(SERVES 6)

My husband loves beetroot, mainly cold and spiced in vinegar with cold meats; this recipe is almost as good!

1 lb (450 g) beetroot
4 tbsp sour cream
2 tbsp wine vinegar
seasoning

Cook the beetroot in boiling, salted water until tender. As soon as you can handle them, peel and dice. Return to the saucepan, add the cream and vinegar and season. Reheat and serve immediately.

GREEN PEAS IN CREAM

(SERVES 4)

The new young fresh green peas of the early summer taste marvellous like this, but the recipe is equally good with frozen peas, giving them extra flavour.

1 lb (450 g) green peas, shelled
3–4 spring onions
4 good sprigs fresh mint
1 tbsp parsley, freshly chopped
1 oz (25 g) butter
2 tbsp flour
2 tsp sugar
1 tsp salt
¼ tsp nutmeg, freshly ground
¼ pt (150 ml) double cream
extra mint for garnish

Blend the butter and flour, then put all ingredients, except the cream, into a saucepan, putting the butter mixture into the centre of the peas and the herbs on top. Pour over ¼ pt (150 ml) boiling water, cover closely and gently simmer for 30 minutes. Stir well and remove the mint and onions and pour on the cream. Bring back to the boil for just 30 seconds and serve immediately garnished with mint sprigs.

HARICOTS VERTS À LA NIÇOISE

(SERVES 4)

1 lb (450 g) small green French beans
2½ oz (65 g) butter
1 small tin peeled Italian tomatoes
1 clove garlic, crushed
salt and pepper
1 dsp tarragon, chopped
1 lemon, peeled with pith removed and cut into wedges

Top and tail beans. If small I leave them whole, otherwise cut into 1 in (2.5 cm) lengths. Boil in salted boiling water for 5 minutes and drain. Meanwhile melt the butter and add tomatoes and juice, garlic, salt and pepper and cook. Add the beans and cook until tender. Add the tarragon and stir well. Pour into a serving dish and decorate with lemon wedges.

GRATIN DAUPHINOIS

(SERVES 4)

This is the first of my favourite potato recipes. It is very Gallic and always a success.

1 lb (450 g) new potatoes (but can be made in winter using old potatoes
¼ pt (150 ml) double cream
8 tbsp grated Gruyère cheese
4 tbsp freshly grated Parmesan cheese (do buy a chunk and grate yourself – you will be amazed at the difference in taste)

Butter well a shallow fireproof gratin dish. Peel and thinly slice the potatoes, drain and thoroughly dry with a tea towel or kitchen roll. Place layers of sliced potatoes in overlapping rows on the bottom of the dish. Pour over about a quarter of the cream, mix the cheeses together and sprinkle 2 tbsp over the cream, dot with butter and season. Continue these layers until dish is full, finishing with a layer of cheese. Dot with butter and cook in a slow oven at about 350 F (180 C) Reg 4 for about 1 hour. If the top starts to get too brown, loosely cover with foil and continue cooking until potatoes are soft. Serve very hot.

NEW POTATOES WITH FENNEL

(SERVES 6)

I have a huge and enthusiastic fennel plant in my herb garden, and I love it, putting it into soups, fish dishes, etc. It is superb with sliced greenhouse tomatoes and mozzarella cheese as a starter, covered with olive oil and sea salt and masses of fennel – and with new potatoes it is a winner.

1½ lb (700 g) new potatoes, preferably small even ones
2 oz (50 g) butter
2 tbsp fennel, freshly chopped

Wash the potatoes and cook in boiling salted water until soft. Drain.

Melt the butter and mix in the potatoes and fennel. If you use large potatoes, when they are cooked slice them while hot into thick rounds and turn these in the butter, taking care not to break them.

LATKES
(Jewish potato cakes)

(SERVES 4)

The children eat these made without onion and with sugar.

4 large raw potatoes, peeled and grated
1 medium Spanish onion, peeled and grated
2 eggs, beaten
2 tbsp flour
½ tsp baking powder
salt, black pepper
butter and oil (I use vegetable) for frying

Combine potatoes and onion in a large bowl. Stir in the egg, the flour and baking powder. Add salt and pepper to taste. Heat some oil and butter in a frying pan and drop in the mixture in spoonfuls. Fry until nicely browned and crisp on the outside and soft on the inside. Drain well and serve. Non onion eaters can either leave it out or substitute a little cheese – but not enough to make the mixture loose.

Salads and Dressings

Have you noticed how salads have changed over the past decade – from the flat, slightly limp lettuce to the marvellous crisp 'iceberg' packed tight and with absolutely no wastage. The glorious abundance of different leaves and fruits available at even the smallest corner greengrocer now means we can do so much more than dish out a bowl of just lettuce, cucumber, tomatoes and radish.

Consider the range. Tomatoes, from the huge firm Dutch ones to the gorgeous tiny cherry tomatoes that my children eat like sweets. Kiwi fruit and mangoes add lovely colour and taste, creamy avocados, Chinese leaves, crunchy fennel and celeriac finely grated and mixed with carrot. Curly endive and red and yellow peppers, chopped into tiny crispy bits; chicory, slightly bitter and lovely with cheese as a change from celery. There's a positive Aladdin's cave to choose from – and all non-fattening!

CUCUMBER AND CHIVE SALAD

(SERVES 6)

It is terribly important to slice the cucumber very thinly, either by hand or try one of those flexible-blade peelers. It takes time to get the knack, but once successful the slices are wonderfully thin.

2 firm good-sized cucumbers, peeled and thinly sliced
salt
2 tsp caster sugar
1 tbsp tarragon vinegar
8 fl oz (225 ml) double cream
fresh black pepper
4 tbsp olive oil
4 tbsp fresh chives, finely chopped (try scissors)

Place wafer-thin cucumbers in a bowl. Sprinkle with salt, cover with a plate and leave for about 1 hour in the fridge. Then put the cucumber into a sieve, rinse quickly and drain well, dabbing with a paper towel. Mix the sugar and vinegar, add the cream and season, then the oil. Add the cucumber and half the chives, put into a glass bowl and sprinkle with the rest of the chives.

WALDORF SALAD

(SERVES 6)

This is my personal favourite, I love the tangy dressing and the crisp 'bite' of the apple and nuts. It is marvellous with any rich meat especially pheasant which, if simply roasted, is quick and easy for that special 'supper for two'. It is perfect, too, for Boxing Day with the cold turkey and ham.

1 lb (450 g) sharp red eating apples
1 tbsp good mayonnaise, Hellmann's or similar
1 tsp caster sugar
2 tbsp lemon juice, freshly squeezed
½ head of celery
2 oz (50 g) shelled walnuts, chopped
¼ pt (150 ml) mayonnaise
1 lettuce

Wash, halve and core the apples. Slice one into thin slices and dice the others dropping them into a bowl of water with lemon to keep their colour. Make a dressing by mixing the 1 tbsp mayonnaise with the caster sugar and lemon juice and dip the sliced apple into the mixture; remove with a slotted spoon and set aside. Toss the diced apple into the dressing and leave to stand for 30 minutes. Finely chop half a sweet white head of the celery, then add this, plus the nuts and the ¼ pt (150 ml) of mayonnaise, mix well to cover all the apple. I serve mine in a shallow glass bowl lined with lettuce leaves and garnish with the sliced apples in a fan shape around the outside.

SUMMER SALAD

(SERVES 4–6)

This is a favourite when the children go strawberry-picking and arrive home, hot, dusty, their mouths stained by strawberry juice and triumphantly carrying baskets of firm lush strawberries! The salad is quite delicious with a moist cold salmon, home-made mayonnaise and tiny Jersey potatoes.

1 lb (450 g) strawberries, hulled and halved
1–2 cucumbers, peeled and sliced
4 kiwi fruit, peeled and sliced
salt and black pepper
2–3 tbsp dry white wine or champagne

On a flat glass or china serving dish I put successive circles of cucumbers, strawberries and kiwi fruit, starting in the centre and working outwards. This must be done just before eating as you do not want too much juice to collect. Season with salt and black pepper and pour over the wine or, for special occasions, champagne. Do not make the mistake of putting the dish in the fridge as the delicate flavour of the strawberries will be lost.

WATERCRESS SALAD

(SERVES 4)

This is one of my sister's recipes. It's delicious with duck or pork fillet.

2 bunches fresh crisp watercress
1 juicy orange
Dressing
3 tbsp olive oil
2 tbsp wine vinegar
1 tbsp lemon juice
1 tbsp curry powder
salt and pepper
1 tsp shallot, finely chopped
little orange juice from orange, above

Wash the watercress, making sure you take out any discoloured leaves and thick stems. Pat dry with a paper towel. Peel the orange, taking off all the white pith and chop into small segments, combine with the watercress in a bowl and cover with clingfilm and refrigerate. To make the dressing, mix all the ingredients well plus any orange juice you manage to collect. Mix in watercress and orange. Make sure all the leaves are covered with the dressing. Cover bowl with clingfilm and chill well before serving.

GRANDPA'S EGG MOUSSE

(SERVES 8)

This is always made at Christmas. Boxing Day cold meat could never be eaten without it.

12 eggs, hard-boiled, shelled and chopped
½ pt (275 ml) mayonnaise
¾ oz (20 g) gelatin (1½ pkts)
¼ pt (150 ml) chicken stock
pinch cayenne pepper
Worcestershire sauce
anchovy essence
salt
¼ pt (150 ml) double cream, lightly whipped
Béchamel sauce (¾ pt/425 ml)
1½ oz (40 g) butter
1½ oz (40 g) flour
¾ pt (425 ml) milk
To decorate
cucumber, thinly sliced
sprigs of watercress

Mix the chopped eggs with the mayonnaise in a bowl. Prepare the Béchamel sauce by mixing all the ingredients together, cover with greaseproof paper to prevent a skin forming, and cool. Dissolve the gelatin in the stock (always add gelatin *to* liquid), melt over gentle heat and, when very smooth, add to the Béchamel sauce. Stir this into the egg and mayonnaise and then season with cayenne pepper, Worcestershire sauce, anchovy essence and salt to taste. When the mousse is cold and thickening, add the cream, folding it in with a metal spoon. Put into a lightly oiled soufflé dish and leave to set in a cool place. Then make a Devil's Sauce to serve with it (see next recipe).

DEVIL'S SAUCE

1 large cup tinned tomatoes, chopped and with cores removed
sugar to taste
1 clove garlic, put through a press, to taste
2 tbsp oil
1 dsp Worcestershire sauce
1 dsp tomato ketchup
salt and pepper

Mix all the ingredients together in list order. The quantities given are enough to go with the Egg Mousse. To serve, turn the mousse onto a flat serving dish and decorate with thin slices of cucumber twisted around the base with sprigs of watercress. Serve the sauce separately.

TOMATO, ORANGE AND CHICORY SALAD

(SERVES 4)

3 firm, fresh heads chicory

4 firm tomatoes

1 large juicy orange

French dressing

Wash, dry and remove any discoloured leaves from chicory and trim the base, slice in half and cut the vee root out. Slice it into strips across. Remove all the skin and pith from the orange, cut into segments making sure you discard any of the white membrane skin. Wash tomatoes and slice thinly. Mix together with the dressing and chill.

ROQUEFORT DRESSING

(SERVES A SALAD FOR 4)

This dressing is lovely on any sort of mixed green salad and combines well with any salad using chunks of chicken.

1½ oz (40 g) Roquefort cheese

4 fl oz (110 ml) soured cream

1 tbsp lemon juice

1 spring onion, finely chopped, white only

Sieve the cheese into a bowl, work in the soured cream and lemon juice little by little until smooth. Add the onion, mix well and chill.

THICK FRENCH DRESSING

(SERVES A SALAD FOR 4)

This dressing, from Maureen Greig, was given to me one night after a particularly long day at the Open Golf Championship at Sandwich, when we arrived exhausted at her house. She served it with salmon, Kentish new potatoes and delicious salad!

½ tsp caster sugar

salt and black pepper

1 clove garlic

1 heaped tsp Dijon mustard

4 tbsp olive oil

2 tbsp wine vinegar

Put the sugar, seasoning and mustard into a bowl that has been rubbed with a clove of garlic. Stir until blended. Slowly add vinegar, stirring all the time. Then blend in the oil until smooth.

TOMATO AND MOZZARELLA SALAD

(SERVES 4)

If you have an abundance of fresh sweet tomatoes in the greenhouse one of the nicest salads is Tomato and Mozzarella. Very good, too, as a simple starter or for lunch on a summer's day with a glass of chilled white wine and plenty of crusty French bread to mop up the juices.

1 lb (450 g) firm sweet tomatoes

8 oz (225 g) Mozzarella cheese

sea salt and freshly milled black pepper

good olive oil (preferably Italian)

1½ tbsp fresh basil, chopped

Simply slice the tomatoes and Mozzarella equally onto the plates. Season with ground sea salt and black pepper and sprinkle oil to taste. Scatter the basil equally between them.

PETER'S FAVOURITE COLESLAW

(SERVES 6)

My husband cannot wait for the winter months with log fires, long evenings when he is in the house because it's too dark to feel guilty about the garden – and jacket potatoes and coleslaw! This recipe started in Leeds, given to me by a friend, and has been added to over the years – you really can put anything in!

½ white cabbage, washed and
  finely shredded

4 sticks celery, washed and chopped

1 large carrot, peeled and rough-grated

2 oz (50 g) sultanas

handful chopped walnuts

2–3 firm tomatoes, rough chopped

1 egg, lightly boiled, shelled
  and chopped

mayonnaise, thinned with the top
  of the milk to a coating consistency

1 clove garlic

seasoning

Toss everything into a bowl previously rubbed around with a garlic clove. Add the mayonnaise, toss and season well with salt and freshly ground black pepper.

PUDDINGS AND DESSERTS

Puddings are, I suppose, to most people the highlight of the meal and generally speaking we all like preparing them. I am no exception, probably because I have three children all with a sweet tooth, which makes it easier to indulge in light creamy concoctions or the lovely old-fashioned steamed puds and nursery desserts of our past. The following are just a few of our favourites.

SCOTTISH FLUMMERY

(SERVES 4)

I first tasted this in Fife, it's very quick to make and has a lovely flavour.

1 tbsp oatmeal
½ pt (275 ml) double cream
3 tbsp clear honey
4 tbsp liqueur whisky
juice of ½ lemon

Heat the oatmeal gently in a heavy-bottomed pan until the mixture turns brown. Set aside. Beat the cream until smooth but not too stiff. Melt the honey in a pan over gentle heat until it runs easily, do not boil. Fold the honey into the cream, stir in the liqueur whisky and the lemon juice. Spoon into individual dishes and serve warm sprinkled with toasted oatmeal.

SYLLABUB

(SERVES 8–10)

Syllabubs are lovely, fruity and very easy sweets, quick to make and always popular.

½ pt (275 ml) double cream
4 oz (110 g) caster sugar
¼ pt (150 ml) sweet white wine
1 large lemon, squeezed and the zest grated very finely
8–10 finger biscuits

Put cream into a basin and then beat in sugar, then wine and lemon juice. Whip until standing in smooth firm peaks, pile into individual dishes and scatter with the peel. Serve with finger biscuits. For a more elaborate version, soak mixed fruit in brandy, first blanching the fruit for 30 seconds in boiling water, draining and drying. Soak in brandy for 30 minutes, then drain fruit and put in the bottom of each dish. It adds a nice bite!

OLD ENGLISH CHRISTMAS SYLLABUB

(SERVES 6–8)

This syllabub is pale pink in colour and very lightly spiced (if you don't like cinnamon, leave it out). As a Christmas pud in tall glasses with holly around the base, it looks super on a buffet table.

8 oz (225 g) red wine

6 tbsp caster sugar

4 in (10 cm) cinnamon stick

8–10 whole cloves

zest from 1 lemon

zest from 1 tangerine

¾ pt (425 ml) double cream

6–8 biscuits

Put the wine, sugar, cinnamon, cloves and lemon and tangerine zest in a saucepan and bring to the boil. Take off the heat and set aside for 24 hours to infuse. Strain the wine into a bowl, then add the cream, whipping continuously until the mixture holds its soft peaks. Put into individual dishes and chill for at least 1½ to 2 hours. Serve with little sponge biscuits, or any dessert biscuit.

BAKED STUFFED PEACHES

(SERVES 4)

Summer peaches, firm, juicy and velvet-skinned – what nicer than eaten fresh? Almost as nice, but much more fattening, is this recipe.

4 peaches halved, skinned and stoned

1 oz (25 g) butter

1 oz (25 g) soft brown sugar

2 oz (50 g) ground almonds

4 cocktail sticks

sprinkling rum and a little extra
   brown sugar

Fill 4 peach cavities with a mixture of the butter, sugar and almonds, top with their other half and pin with a cocktail stick. Place them to fit closely in a buttered shallow ovenproof dish and cover with brown sugar and a liberal sprinkle of rum. Bake in a moderate oven until brown, about 20 minutes. You may need to baste to prevent the tops drying out. Serve very hot with thick double cream.

RUM CHOCOLATE MOUSSE

(SERVES 8–10)

A phenomenally smooth, rich dessert that is quick to make.

1½ oz (40 g) sugar

2–4 tbsp rum

4 oz (110 g) dark chocolate
   (Rowntree or Terrys)

2–3 tbsp whipping cream

2 stiffly beaten egg whites

½ pt (275 ml) whipped cream

Over a low heat, simmer the sugar and rum until dissolved. Meanwhile melt the chocolate in a basin over hot water; when it is smooth stir in the whipping cream. Add the syrup to the chocolate and stir until smooth. When mixture is cool, fold into it the stiffly beaten egg whites. Then gently fold in the whipped cream and serve in individual dishes.

CRÈME BRÛLÉE

(SERVES 6)

Everyone's favourite, with the lovely crunchy top and the layer of smooth cream underneath. There are many different recipes, and this one is very simple.

5 egg yolks

1 tbsp caster sugar

1 pt (575 ml) fresh double cream

few drops vanilla essence

demerara sugar

Mix the yolks with the sugar and whisk until fluffy. Heat the cream and vanilla to blood heat over a basin of water and then pour onto egg mixture. Strain into a wet shallow fireproof dish and cook in a bain-marie until set. Allow 30 minutes at 325 F (160 C) Reg 3. Allow to cool and then cover with a 1 in (2–3 cm) layer of demerara sugar, put the grill on high and grill until the sugar melts. Take care not to burn. Cool and the top turns into a lovely smooth crispy toffee.

NÈGRE EN CHEMISE

(SERVES 8–10)

This is a lovely dinner party pud, found many years ago in a Cordon Bleu cookery course. Very rich, so you only need to serve very small portions. The praline makes a lovely bitey texture against the smooth richness of the chocolate. I very often serve a bowl of mango at the same time, cutting the fruit into slices and serving just 2 or 3 per person with the chocolate.

12 oz (350 g) block good dark chocolate

about 4 fl oz (110 ml) water

3 oz (75 g) butter, unsalted

4 oz (110 g) praline (see recipe below)

brandy, to taste

8 fl oz (225 ml) double cream

8 fl oz (225 ml) double cream to decorate

First prepare your bombe mould if you have one, if not use a Pyrex 1 pt (575 ml) basin, lightly oiled. Break up the chocolate and put into a basin with the water. Put the basin over a saucepan half-filled with water and melt gently until a thick cream is reached. Draw on one side and cool. Meanwhile cream the butter, add the cooled chocolate and gradually beat in the praline. Flavour with brandy. Whip 8 oz (225 ml) cream, cut and fold into mixture and then pour into your mould. Leave to set for 2–3 hours. Turn out by dipping the basin quickly into hot water to loosen the edges. Whip the remaining cream and pipe rosettes in a ruff around the bottom. If you are clever make some large flat chocolate rounds, by melting down chocolate and then covering a sheet of baking paper with the liquid chocolate, put on in teaspoonfuls and ease out to make small circles. Leave to set and then carefully peel the backing paper. Otherwise decorate with Cadbury's buttons which look just as effective.

Praline

4 oz (110 g) blanched almonds

4 oz (110 g) sugar

Put the blanched almonds and sugar into a thick-bottomed pan over a low heat. Stir all the time until the sugar has caramelized and the almonds are toasted. It should be a pale brown; watch that it does not get too dark – it turns very quickly. Pour into an oiled tin plate or enamelled surface and spread it to a thin layer. When completely cold and hard, break into bits and put into the toughest plastic bag you have and roll or pound with a rolling pin. This should produce a crumb-like texture. This keeps well for a month in an airtight jar.

CHOCOLATE ROULADE

(SERVES 8)

The classic party sweet of which so many people say, 'It seems so difficult – all that sponge!' In fact it is so easy, and I make it for my children for Sunday lunch.

8 oz (225 g) caster sugar
5 eggs, separated
6 oz (175 g) block good plain chocolate
3–4 tbsp water
fresh whipped cream

Put the sugar in a bowl and gradually add the egg yolks, beating all the time until the mixture is pale and lemony-coloured. Melt the broken-up chocolate in 2–3 tbsp of water in a basin set over a pan of water. Do not let the bottom pan boil. When it is a thick cream, put the pan aside. Whip egg whites to a firm snow, then add the chocolate to the egg mixture and cut and fold the whites into this mixture. Pour it into a large shallow swiss roll tin lined with oiled greaseproof paper, pop into a pre-set oven at 350 F (180 C) Reg 4 and cook for 10–15 minutes until firm to touch. The top will go crisp and will rise up over the sides – but just check that the inside is set; if not, leave for a few more minutes. Have ready a clean tea towel wrung out in cold water. Take out the roulade and cover with the cold damp cloth and leave for 12 hours in a cool place.

When you are ready to use the roulade, put another cloth or greaseproof paper onto a worktop, cover with icing sugar and upturn the roulade (minus its cloth) onto it. Carefully remove the lining paper and then fill with fresh whipped cream, either plain or flavoured with brandy, run or vanilla. I often roll up fruit as well, fresh strawberries, blackcurrants (delicious) or raspberries. Roll up using the cloth or paper – don't worry if it cracks, pop a long flat serving plate at the back and roll it up on to the dish. I put vine leaves under mine or decorate with fruit, or tiny flowers. At Christmas a Father Christmas on his sleigh rides across the top, with reindeers and holly.

CHOCOLATE CHESTNUT CREAM

(SERVES 4)

This is a rich dessert and gloriously fattening, so ration yourself strictly to one a week!

4 oz (110 g) chocolate (plain Bournville)
½ oz (15 g) butter
1 egg yolk
8¾ oz (245 ml) tin sweetened chestnut purée
2 tbsp brandy
½ pt (275 ml) double cream

Melt the chocolate with the butter in a basin over hot, not boiling water. Remove when smooth and add beaten egg yolk. Beat in chestnut purée, first mashing down with a fork if it seems solid. Add brandy, whip

Calves' Liver in Citrus Sauce
Pears St Moritz

the cream and fold into the mixture. Pour into a glass bowl and decorate with piped cream and curls of chocolate.

FLUFFY LEMON CHEESECAKE

(SERVES 8)

A very lemony fresh cheesecake. The children love it because of the chocolate digestive biscuit base.

packet dark chocolate digestive biscuits
3–4 tbsp butter, melted
3 packets 3 oz (75 g) Phili cheese
3 tbsp caster sugar
1 tsp vanilla essence
juice and grated rind of 1 large lemon
2 egg yolks, beaten
½ oz (15 g) gelatin (1 packet)
3 egg whites
½ pt (275 ml) double cream

To make the base, crush the biscuits and mix with the melted butter, then press into a loose-bottomed flan case and cook for 5 minutes. For the filling, combine in a bowl the cheese, sugar and vanilla essence, mix until smooth. Add lemon juice and rind and beaten egg yolks and whisk until smooth. Dissolve the gelatin in 2 tbsp warm water and, making sure it is well dissolved, add slowly to the mixture, stirring all the time to prevent lumps. Beat egg whites until firm, fold into mixture and then fold in the cream, whipped but not too stiff. Put this mixture into the crust and chill. I decorate by piping cream round the edge and grating plain chocolate over the whole thing.

Nègre en Chemise
Fresh Green Fruit Salad

PETER'S FAVOURITE 'LEEDS' CHEESECAKE

(SERVES 8)

When we first went to Leeds we spent many hours in the Bellow household. Carol and Marshall were marvellously hospitable and this was Carol's cheesecake which used to greet us home, hot, dirty and tired after battling with our builders at Blackmore Farm.

7½ oz (215 g) packet digestive biscuits
3 oz (75 g) butter, melted
1¼ lb (560 g) cream cheese (full fat)
1 cup sugar
1 oz (25 g) butter, melted
2 egg whites, stiffly whipped
2 egg yolks
1 tbsp cornflour
4 oz (110 g) double cream
1–2 tsp vanilla essence and whatever you choose to add: cherries, raisins, nuts, etc.

To make the base, crush the biscuits and mix them with the 3 oz melted butter. Press into a loose-bottomed flan case and cook in oven for 5 minutes. For the filling, whip the egg whites and once stiff add all other ingredients (I add raisins to the basic recipe) and stir until smooth. Pour mixture into cooled base and cook for 1 hour in a low oven at 225 F (110 C) Reg ¼. It will still be loose. Turn off oven and leave in for a further hour. Carol also adapted this recipe by putting no fruit into the mixture, making a plain sponge base and when cooked and cool topping with soured cream.

CHEESECAKE WILLIAMS

(SERVES 12)

This makes a huge cheesecake, ideal for a supper party or a weekend with all the family around. Use a large 10 in (25 cm) spring-sided loose-bottomed ring about 2½ in (6 cm) deep. The base and filling, when made, freeze well, and you just add the topping when needed. Janet Williams and I produced our first-born together and this was always on the table for mums at nursery teas!

10 oz (275 g) digestive biscuits
4 oz (110 g) butter, melted
2 lb (900 g) cottage cheese
¼ pt (150 ml) single cream
6 oz (175 g) caster sugar
1 tsp lemon juice
2 x 3 oz (75 g) packets cream cheese (Phili)
5 eggs
2 tsp vanilla essence

To make the base, crush the biscuits and mix with the melted butter, then press into the bottom of the ring, put in the oven for 5 minutes then set aside to cool. For the filling, put the cheese, eggs and cream into blender and mix until smooth. Stir in lemon juice, vanilla and sugar. Mix well. Cook for 1–1¼ hours at about 350 F (180 C) Reg 4 until set (just), remove from oven and leave to cool. For the topping use either fresh fruit with the juice thickened with arrowroot, or 2 tins of fruit filling, e.g. apricot, cherry or blackcurrant.

COFFEE AND GINGER BOMBE

(SERVES 6–8)

A love, call it addiction, to ice cream led me to search out ice cream recipes. The beauty of this particular pud is that it adapts to whichever fruit is in season and any flavour of ice cream.

Meringue
3 egg whites
6 oz (175 g) caster sugar
Filling
½ pt (275 ml) double cream
1 jar preserved ginger – drain and chop the ginger into small pieces
Base
coffee ice cream (1 litre pack)

If you have a bombe mould, use that; I personally use a 2 pt (1.1 l) Pyrex bowl. To make the meringue, whisk the whites until very stiff and in peaks, add 3 tbsp caster sugar, one at a time, beating for 1 minute between each addition. Fold in the remainder. Prepare lightly oiled baking paper, the non-stick type, and then pipe or use the back of a spoon to make three circles to fit your bowl, e.g. one small, one medium, 1 larger for the top; make undersize rather than too-generous circles. Bake in a cool oven at 250 F (125 C) Reg ½ until crisp, pale biscuity-coloured and dry. Next, for the filling, whip the cream, drain and chop the ginger and add to the cream. Set this mixture aside. Then comes the not-so-easy bit! Leave the ice cream out to soften. When just soft and pliable, not liquidy, smooth it, bit by bit, starting on the bottom round your mould. It's easier if you put the mould in the freezer for a while to get it very cold. Don't worry if it doesn't look too immaculate. Starting at the bottom, put a spoonful of the cream mixture in and cover with the smallest circle of meringue, add more cream/ginger, then the second layer, more cream/ginger and put in the third layer (if these are too big, trim the edges with a sharp knife). Finish with a layer of ice cream to seal the bombe and put into the freezer until needed. Defrost for about 30 minutes before using; if the mould sticks apply a hot cloth round it before upending into a serving dish. I surround mine with a little of the ginger syrup.

COEUR À LA CRÈME

(SERVES 6)

If you have them, the tiny white china moulds with little holes are lovely, if not use ramekin dishes. Thanks to all my kids I have a surfeit of muslin nappies, boiled and reboiled and put away for jam straining, curd straining and Coeur à la Crème! Line the mould with muslin first.

3 oz (75 g) cream cheese
3 oz (75 g) cottage cheese
3 oz (75 g) icing sugar
3 oz (75 g) double cream (very fresh) or plain yoghurt
3 egg whites
Purée
large punnet raspberries or strawberries
icing sugar, optional
liqueur, optional

Sieve the cream cheese, cottage cheese, icing sugar and cream into a basin through a fine nylon mesh. Stiffly whisk the egg whites and fold into mixture. Pour into moulds, fold muslin over top and leave in fridge. The whey should run out of them. To make the purée, put fruit into blender and mix until liquid, add icing sugar if needed and liqueur if liked to flavour. Sieve if no pips required. To serve, turn out into dessert plates and surround with fresh raspberry purée or strawberry purée and the fruits themselves. Gorgeous for a summer dinner party – a sprig of orange blossom on each plate.

EARL GREY TEA PARFAIT

(SERVES 6–8)

In my mind, one of the most impressive frozen desserts is a parfait, creamy smooth and made with the freshest cream, with flavours such as brandy, coffee or chestnut. My favourite is the following recipe from the kitchens of the Turnberry Hotel. Fairly easy to make, it is deliciously different with its delicate flavour of Earl Grey tea.

6 Earl Grey tea bags
8 fl oz (225 ml) boiling water
juice of ½ lemon
4 egg yolks
5 oz (150 g) soft brown sugar
½ pt (275 ml) whipped cream
Tea Sauce
½ pt (275 ml) tea, cold
juice of 1 lemon
4 oz (110 g) caster sugar

Infuse together for 5 minutes tea bags, boiling water and lemon juice. Put into bain marie and thicken slightly, stirring constantly. It takes about 20 minutes – take care not to boil. Leave until cold then fold in cream, whipped until thick and fluffy but not stiff. Pour into rectangular non-stick cake tin or other suitable mould and freeze for 12 hours. To make sauce, put all ingredients into a pan, heat to 230 F (115 C) Reg ¼ and leave until cold. This mixture should be at the syrup stage. If not, then add a little sugar and reheat to 230 F (115 C) Reg ¼.

To serve, dip the parfait tin quickly into hot water or put a hot cloth on the outside. When loose, turn out onto dish and surround with some of the sauce. Serve the rest of the sauce separately. To complete the picture you can decorate with tiny sprigs of green and tiny flowers.

SAN FRANCISCAN SOURED CREAM FLAN WITH APRICOT SAUCE

(SERVES 6)

Having first eaten this in San Francisco, I searched high and low for a recipe and drew a blank until I came across this one by Denis Curtis. Now I often make it.

6 oz (175 g) shortcrust pastry
3 eggs, separated
5 oz (150 g) caster sugar
8 oz (225 g) sultanas, finely chopped
¼ tsp ground cloves
¼ tsp salt
5 oz (150 g) soured cream
grated rind of 1 lemon
Apricot sauce
tinned apricots or dried apricots
juice of 1 lemon
splash apricot liqueur

Roll out pastry and line a 9 in (23 cm) flan ring or a baking tray. Beat the egg yolks with the sugar until pale yellow and nicely thick. Mix the sultanas, spice and salt into the yolk mixture. Add the soured cream and lemon rind. Beat egg whites until firm and standing in peaks. Fold into mixture and spoon into the base. Bake at 425 F (220 C) Reg 7 for 15 minutes, lowering it to 350 F (180 C) Reg 4 for another 20 minutes until firm to the touch and lightly golden. Leave in the ring to 'rest' before removing rim. To make the apricot sauce, either strain the tinned apricot and blend or soak the dried ones and place in a blender, add the lemon juice and a splash of liqueur to flavour. Serve the sauce separately to pour around the slice of flan.

ALMOND MERINGUE WITH RASPBERRIES

(SERVES 8)

Meringue is always popular, a bit like chocolate, and this pud is no exception. A variation on using hazelnuts, the almond mixture is super and it makes a perfect buffet party dessert. Try, for a change, topping it with sliced mango or kiwi fruit.

4 egg whites

9 oz (250 g) caster sugar

3–4 drops of vanilla essence

½ tsp vinegar

4½ oz (125 g) ground almonds

½ pt (275 ml) double cream

8 oz (225 g) raspberries

Cover a large flat baking tray with silicone paper. Set oven at 375 F (190 C) Reg 5. Whisk egg whites until stiff, add the sugar 1 tbsp at a time and continue beating until mixture is very stiff and stands in peaks. Whisk in vanilla essence and vinegar and fold in the almonds. Spoon the mixture into a large circle about 10 in (25 cm) in diameter and a good ½ in (1 cm) thick. Cook for about 30 minutes. The top should be crispy and the inside soft rather like a marshmallow. Take out and, holding a cooling rack over the top, flip over. You can leave it overnight or use immediately, in which case once the meringue has cooked, whip the cream and pile it on top and then top that with raspberries or any fruit of your choice.

FRESH GREEN FRUIT SALAD

(SERVES 8)

A green fruit salad, as opposed to one with mixed fruit, looks cool and interesting, particularly after a rich meal.

3 green dessert apples, peeled, cored and diced (put into lemon water to prevent browning)

4 kiwi fruit, sliced

8 oz (225 g) green grapes, de-pipped and halved (skinned if you have the patience)

3 green figs, cut into dice

3 pears, peeled, halved, cored and diced

small tin lychees, left in halves

green-fleshed melon (i.e. Honeydew) scooped out with melon-baller

Syrup

4 oz (110 g) caster sugar

½ pt (275 ml) water

slice lemon peel

1–2 drops green colouring

splash Grand Marnier, optional

Arrange the fruit in the serving bowl. Make the syrup from the caster sugar and water, pop a piece of lemon peel in it and bring slowly to the boil, simmer for 5 minutes, strain and cool. Add 1–2 drops of green colouring, pour over fruit and chill well. Add liqueur (Grand Marnier) if you wish.

COINTREAU SOUFFLÉ

(SERVES 4)

This is lovely for a special family supper when it doesn't matter if you disappear into the kitchen. At a more formal dinner party you need someone else out there after the main course to put together and cook the soufflé.

½ pt (275 ml) milk

3 large eggs, separated

2 oz (50 g) caster sugar

finely grated zest of 2 oranges

1 oz (25 g) flour

4 tbsp Cointreau

2 additional egg whites

1 tbsp icing sugar

Bring the milk to the boil and set aside. Beat the egg yolks with half the caster sugar and the orange zest until the mixture is thick and pale yellow. Whisk in the flour, followed by the hot milk. Pour mixture back into the pan and bring up to a simmer, whisking constantly. Continue for 2 minutes then take off heat and cool a little before adding Cointreau. Whisk egg whites until they are stiff, add the remaining caster sugar and whip until the mixture is glossy. Fold lightly into custard mixture until blended. Pour into individual cocotte dishes, cook in a preheated oven at 425 F (220 C) Reg 7 for 8–10 minutes, then dust with icing sugar and serve immediately.

FRAISES À LA CRÈME

(SERVES 4–5)

I look forward to the strawberry season and pray each year for a bumper crop. They are so versatile, from plates of firm sweet berries on their own to puddings such as the one below. There are masses of 'pick your own' around us and it's one of the children's great delights to go picking, although I swear they eat as many as they put into their baskets.

1 lb (450 g) firm dry strawberries, hulled and gently wiped with a damp cloth
4 tbsp caster sugar
4 tbsp Curaçao or Grand Marnier
½ pt (275 ml) double cream
2 dry macaroons

Put strawberries in a wide serving bowl and sprinkle with the sugar.

Cover and leave in a cool place (not the fridge) for 1 hour. Pour the liqueur over them, cover and leave for a further 2 hours, or until required. Whip the cream until fairly thick (not solid, sweeten to taste if required) and crumble in the macaroons. Pour this mixture carefully over the strawberries and mix very carefully with two forks, just turning them so that the fruit is not crushed. Serve immediately. I use a wide shallow glass bowl and put tiny strawberry leaves around the sides just before serving.

GREEK PUDDING

(SERVES 6)

This pudding is delicious served in the summer with strawberries or raspberries and in the winter with hot apple or apricot purée. I can't remember where it came from. I suspect I got it out of a magazine at the hairdressers. A very easy-going man, my hairdresser knows my addiction to unusual recipes and keeps an old pair of scissors handy!

1 pt (575 ml) whipping or double cream
2 standard cartons plain natural yoghurt
2 drops vanilla essence
5 oz (150 g) dark brown soft sugar

Whip the cream until stiff but not too hard, fold in the yoghurts and vanilla essence and put into a large pudding dish. Sprinkle the dark brown sugar all over the top about ¼ in (5 mm) thick and put in the fridge for several hours before serving.

MANGO AND ORANGE GÂTEAU

(SERVES 6–8)

With its deep orange flesh brimming with juice, the mango is without doubt one of the most versatile and delicious of our imported fruits. We eat masses of it in Antigua each January on holiday – the island is lovely, unspoilt on the windward side – long empty beaches, coconuts and other exotic fruit in abundance. I put mango on veal, a change from orange, with chicken and a delicious cold mango and orange soup. I chop it into salads –the children love it – and as an expensive but gorgeous starter I put slices on a plate with fresh shredded crabmeat and a delicately flavoured mayonnaise. This pud is three layers of orange-flavoured sponge sandwiched together with fresh mango and cream.

4 eggs
4 oz (110 g) caster sugar
zest of orange, finely grated (choose one with a bright orange skin)
4 oz (110 g) flour, sifted
juice of ½ orange, strained
¾ oz (20 g) butter, melted and cooled
Filling
2 medium-sized ripe mangoes
½ pt (275 ml) double cream
2 tbsp caster sugar
2–3 tbsp Grand Marnier
icing sugar

Prepare a swiss roll tin 9 in x 13 in (23 cm x 33 cm). Brush lightly with butter and line with silicone paper, or greaseproof brushed with butter. Whisk the eggs and sugar and orange zest until creamy and thick. Carefully fold in the flour, alternating with the orange juice and melted butter. Pour mixture into tin and bake at 400 F (200 C) Reg 6 for about 12–15 minutes until golden brown and spongy to touch. To make the filling, carefully peel the mangoes with a sharp knife, cut the flesh away from the stone and dice into small chunks. Whip the double cream and caster sugar until fairly stiff and then fold in the mango. When the sponge has cooled, remove the lining paper, trim the edges and then cut crossways into three equal rectangles. Sprinkle a little Grand Marnier over each. Spread half the mango cream over the first slice and top with the second. Spread this with the rest of the filling and top with the third sponge. Sprinkle icing sugar over the top and garnish with pretty flowers; violets look lovely.

SUSSEX POND PUDDING

(SERVES 6)

We had a few laughs over this one – I had never come across it until Jean Michelmore gave me the recipe. I couldn't believe it would work and eventually amid laughter we set aside an afternoon and did it. Well, I take it all back, it is mouthwateringly gooey and delicious – lovely for a simple meal as it is very filling. Jean actually said that her mother used to make it in the Thirties, since when her children have been ceaselessly fighting the flab. So draw your own conclusion!

8 oz (225 g) self-raising flour
¼ tsp salt
4 oz (110 g) shredded suet
4 fl oz (110 ml) iced water
Filling
4 oz (110 g) butter, diced
1 large lemon (choose a large thin-skinned one)
4 oz (110 g) demerara sugar

Sift the flour and salt into a basin. Add the shredded suet and mix lightly with a fork to distribute it evenly. Make a well in the centre of the flour and add the iced water, little by little, to make a soft dough. Mix with a knife (you may not need all the water). Knead the dough lightly on a floured surface until it is smooth and free from cracks and roll out to a thickness of about ¼ in (5 mm). Cut a quarter segment and set aside for the lid. Use the remainder to line a well-buttered pudding basin of 1½ pt (850 ml) capacity. Dampen the edges of the join to make a seal. For the filling, put half the diced butter in the bottom of the basin, prick the lemon all over with a skewer and sit it firmly upright in the butter, cover it with the sugar and remaining butter. Roll out the remaining dough for a lid. Dampen the edges and gently press it into place, cover the basin with a layer of greaseproof paper which has been folded to make a 1 in (2.5 cm) pleat across the diameter of the basin, tie on tightly with string. Then top it all with foil, leaving it loose over the top and well down the sides. Stand the basin in a saucepan and pour in boiling water to come halfway up its sides. Cover the pan and simmer for 3 hours. Check the water from time to time and top up with boiling water; do not let pudding go off the boil. Rest the pudding for a moment before turning out into a dish which is deep enough to contain the river of golden goo which floods out when you cut the first slice – and make sure everyone gets a slice of lemon. Serve with thick cream.

SALLY'S CREAM

(SERVES 4–6)

My sister is a good cook and usually prefers savouries with lots of herbs and spices to desserts. But this is one pudding that she admits being addicted to. It is a scrumptious mixture of cream, lemon and almonds in a rum-soaked sponge. It came, years ago, from a newspaper cutting and is appropriately called Sally's Cream.

2 fl oz (60 ml) Jamaica rum
1 fl oz (30 ml) milk
7 or 8 small sponge cakes (the quantity depends on the size of the bowl you are using)
peel (finely grated) and juice of 1 lemon
1 pt (575 ml) double cream
4 oz (110 g) sugar
1 oz (25 g) flaked almonds

Mix the rum and milk together, slice the sponge cakes lengthways then soak them in the mixture. Into a double saucepan put the lemon peel and the cream. Make it scalding hot but *do not let it boil*. Add sugar and reheat then add lemon juice (again, do not boil). Remove from the stove and stir all the time until the cream is nearly cold. Line the bowl with the sponge cakes and very carefully pour in the cream over the cakes and then put in the fridge to chill. When the pudding is set, toast the almonds and sprinkle over the top.

FAVOURITE BAKEWELL

(SERVES 8)

This next recipe came from a dear lady who babysat for me when I first arrived in Surrey. It then became a firm favourite with our youngest son's godfather, 'Uncle Jack' Buchanan, who requests it every time he comes for Sunday lunch. Serve it with thick cream.

6 oz (175 g) rich shortcrust pastry
Filling
4 oz (110 g) butter
4 oz (110 g) sugar
1 egg
4 oz (110 g) ground rice or semolina
1 tsp vanilla or almond essence
1 heaped tbsp red jam

Line an 8 in (20 cm) flan tin with the shortcrust pastry and set aside. Melt the butter and add sugar and stir till melted over low heat. Remove from heat and add the rice, beaten egg and flavouring. Stir well. Line the bottom of the pastry case with the jam and then fill with the mixture, put into baking oven at about 375 F (190 C) Reg 5 for 20 minutes and lower the heat to finish off.

CHERYL'S PASSION FRUIT MOUSSE

(SERVES 8–10)

We met Cheryl and her husband, Ian, in Antigua on holiday. Wandering along the deserted beach one day, discussing our interests, I discovered that she too loved cooking and, coming from South Africa, used lots of fruit in her puds. Months later, back in England, they came for dinner and she arrived clutching a tub of Passion Fruit Mousse. It is delicious and has rapidly become a favourite.

1 cup caster sugar
1 cup cold water
12 passion fruits, plus 1 or 2 extra fruits for decoration
2 dsp cornflour, mixed to a paste with 1–2 tsp cold water
1 lemon jelly
4 egg whites
8 fl (225 ml) double cream

Heat the sugar and water and bring to the boil, do not stir. Add passion fruit pulp and boil until flesh separates from the pips. Remove from heat and put through sieve. Add the cornflour mixture and cook for a minute or two. Add the lemon jelly squares and dissolve. Take off heat and cool. Stiffly beat the egg whites and set aside then beat the cream until holding its shape but not too firm. Fold the passion fruit mixture into the cream and lastly fold in the egg whites. If liked, then add the pulp plus pips from the extra fruit. Pour into mould and allow to set.

PEARS GRILLED WITH HONEY

(SERVES 4)

We first tasted pears grilled with honey and local liqueur in France. I remember thinking how simple and wondering why we go to such lengths with our own desserts. After a full meal the freshness of fruit seems so natural. My five-year-old adores this recipe.

4 large juicy William pears
juice of 1 lemon
1 oz (25 g) unsalted Normandy butter
4 fl oz (110 ml) double cream
1 rounded tbsp clear honey
1 rounded tbsp brown sugar

Wash and dry the pears. Cut in half lengthways and scoop out the core with a teaspoon to make a cavity. Rub the cut surface with lemon juice. Melt the butter and brush the cut slices with it. Arrange the pears cut side down in a baking dish and pour the rest of the lemon juice over the pears. Whip the cream and chill. Put the grill onto maximum. Put the pears under grill far enough from the element not to burn and grill for about 8 minutes. Turn them over and brush again with butter and fill the hollows with honey, sprinkle with the sugar (fairly quickly) and put back under the grill until brown on top and bubbling. Allow to cool for a few minutes, then put a spoonful of cream into the hollow of each pear. Serve warm. For a change try the same with fresh peaches.

PEARS ST MORITZ

(SERVES 4)

Another pear recipe, this is one of Michael Gill's from Pool Court. Best in summer when raspberries are plentiful, it takes a little time to prepare but is well worth the effort.

8 small pears, with stalks left on
Poaching liquid
1 pt (575 ml) sugar syrup, made from 20 oz (560 g) granulated or cube sugar brought to the boil on 1 pt (575 ml) water
1 pt (575 ml) white wine
2 lemons
½ stick cinnamon
6 cloves
6 peppercorns
Pear mousse
3 egg yolks
3 oz (75 g) caster sugar
2½ leaves gelatin
1½ fl oz (40 ml) Poire William Eau de Vie
¼ pt (150 ml) double cream
4 egg whites
Raspberry sauce
8 oz (225 g) raspberries
juice of 3 lemons
2 tbsp icing sugar
1 tbsp Framboise Eau de Vie

Peel four of the pears, being careful to leave the stalks on. Hollow out the core from the base of the pear to produce a cavity large enough to pipe the mousse into. Put prepared pears into cold water and lemon juice to prevent discoloration. Add the ingredients for the poaching liquid to a 3–4 pt (1.7–2.25 l) pan, bring to the boil and add the well-drained pears making sure that they are completely covered. Cover with a piece of greaseproof paper cut to the same size as the pan. Leave to simmer for about 10 minutes until cooked but remaining firm. Place on a tray and leave to cool. Repeat these two processes for the remaining four pears; the pan will not hold more than four at a time. To make the mousse, place the egg yolks and sugar into a bowl and whisk together over a pan of simmering water until the mixture leaves 'whisk marks'. Take off the heat and add the pre-soaked gelatin and the Poire William. Whisk well and leave to one side until almost set. Whip the cream to soft peaks and fold into the egg mixture. Whip egg whites to stiff peaks and again fold into the mixture. Leave to set in the fridge. Make the raspberry sauce by liquidizing the raspberries, lemon juice and icing sugar together. Strain, using a fine sieve. Finally stir in the Framboise. When the mousse has set, put into a piping bag fitted with a plain nozzle and pipe into the cavity. Smooth off using a palette knife. Place the filled pears on to individual plates and lightly coat with the raspberry sauce. Garnish with a piece of mint and a few fresh raspberries. If you have any mousse left over, offer separately as an additional sweet.

BANANA MERINGUE

(SERVES 4)

Lynn and Barry Took are old friends and many's the happy evening we have had in their company. His marvellous sense of humour matches my husband's and we are guaranteed more than a few laughs. Lynn cooked us this simple but delicious pudding.

6 bananas
2 oz (50 g) butter
1 tsp ground cinnamon
3 eggs
2 oz (50 g) soft brown sugar
1 tbsp rum
3 oz (75 g) caster sugar

Cut the bananas in half and then split each half lengthwise. Fry in butter until golden brown then place in a lightly buttered ovenproof dish and sprinkle with cinnamon. Separate the eggs and put yolks in a bowl over a saucepan of hot water. Add the brown sugar and heat gently, stirring until the mixture thickens. Do not allow to boil. Stir in the rum and pour mixture over bananas. Whisk the egg whites until stiff and fold in the caster sugar. Pile on top of ingredients in dish and bake in oven at 325 F (160 C) Reg 3 for 35 minutes until the meringue is browned.

BANOFFI PIE

(SERVES 6–8)

I only have to hear someone say Banoffi Pie and I'm immediately transported back to Yorkshire, and always The Spice Box restaurant. It was here, some 12 to 14 years ago, that I first tasted this pie and it was several years before I managed to acquire the recipe.

1 large tin condensed milk

6 oz (175 g) digestive biscuits

1 oz (25 g) butter

2 bananas, mashed

5 fl oz (150 ml) whipping cream

little coffee essence

grated chocolate, to decorate

Put the tin of condensed milk into a pan of boiling water, immersing completely. The tin should not be opened or pierced in any way. Boil the tin for 3 hours, making sure that the water in the pan is kept topped up. Meanwhile make a biscuit base by crushing the biscuits and adding the butter, melted, to bind them together. Line an 8 in (20 cm) flan dish with this. When the tin has cooled down a little, open it and spread the caramelized milk over the base. It should be a rich toffee colour. Allow to cool. Spread mashed banana over this and top with whipped cream flavoured with a little coffee essence. Decorate with grated chocolate.

WHITE TRUFFLES

(SERVES 12)

Lovely made for Christmas and piled up on a small-stemmed plate with sprigs of holly or mistletoe.

4 oz (110 g) unsalted butter

8 oz (225 g) white chocolate

1 fl oz (30 ml) Cointreau or other liqueur to taste

1 lb (450 g) white coating chocolate

Beat butter until soft and creamy. Melt the 8 oz (225 g) chocolate in a double boiler (taking care that the water does not boil) and pour into the butter. Add the liqueur and beat mixture until thick and white. Place into a piping bag with ¼ in (5 mm) round nozzle and pipe into balls on a piece of foil. Allow to set in the refrigerator before dipping in the coating chocolate.

AMERICAN GELATIN CHEESECAKE

(SERVES 12)

One of my American recipes from San Diego and the Crow family. It makes a lovely big fluffy cheesecake and can be topped with fresh fruit or soured cream.

4 oz (110 g) butter, melted

6 oz (175 g) digestive biscuits, crumbled

2 oz (50 g) ground almonds

2 tbsp sugar

4 egg yolks

4 oz (110 g) sugar

¼ tsp salt

⅓ cup milk

vanilla essence

2 packets gelatin

½ cup water

juice 1 lemon

1½ lb (675 g) soft cream cheese

4 egg whites

3 oz (75 g) sugar

4 oz (110 g) whipping cream

To make the base mix together the melted butter, digestive biscuits, ground almonds and sugar, press into a deep 10 in x 3 in (25 cm x 7.5 cm) deep spring-sided flan ring and set aside. For the filling, beat the egg yolks with the sugar and salt. Add the milk gradually and a few drops of vanilla essence. Heat the custard mixture over a pan of hot water, stir until it starts to thicken. Soak the gelatin in half a cup of water. Stir into the hot custard until dissolved (make sure it is dissolved). Cool the custard and then add the lemon juice and soft cream cheese (work this first with a fork to get it smooth). Stir until well blended. Whip the egg whites until stiff and fold in gradually. Add the 3 oz (75 g) sugar and beat until stiff and then fold in the whipping cream. Fill the flan case and chill well in the refrigerator.

ENGADINA

(SERVES 6)

Frensham Ponds Hotel is our 'local'; sitting on the side of Frensham Big Pond, it is always popular particularly for Sunday lunch. This is a house speciality as are the White Truffles.

12 oz sweet shortcrust pastry
8 oz (225 g) walnut pieces
6 oz (175 g) caster sugar
5 fl oz (150 ml) water
8 fl oz (225 ml) double cream
½ oz (15 g) clear honey
8 oz (225 g) dark coating chocolate
8 half walnuts

Take an 8 in (20 cm) round flan tin with a removable base, line it with pastry and fill with the walnut pieces. Combine the sugar and water and dissolve over a low heat until sugar is completely dissolved. Increase heat and boil sugar to a light caramel taking care that the sugar crystals do not form on the sides of the pan. Add cream immediately, then the honey, stir to combine then continue to boil rapidly for a further 8–10 minutes. (The timing will determine the caramel. Increase for a firmer caramel, decrease for a softer one. I suggest that you go for the softer one the first time of making and increase timings from there.) Pour caramel over the nuts and tap the flan case to remove any air trapped. Allow to cool, then cover with a well pricked piece of pastry sealing the edges well. Place on a pastry tray and bake for 30–40 minutes in a moderate oven or until pastry is golden brown. Melt the coating chocolate over hot water and, when smooth, coat the top of the engadina and decorate with the walnut halves.

N.B. Do not refrigerate as this has a tendency to crystalize the caramel.

Cakes and Biscuits

One of my strongest childhood memories is the smell of scones cooking when I came home from school. Is anything more scrummy than piping-hot scones with the butter dripping off them and a big blob of home-made strawberry jam in the middle?

We much prefer homemade cakes and biscuits and 'P.J.', who looks after us, is a lovely down-to-earth lady who cooks farmhouse fare which disappears almost as quickly as it is produced, hot and succulent from the Aga. It really is a wonder we are not all 12 stone and dieting. The following are a few of our traditional and favourite recipes.

CHRISTMAS CAKE

My mother always made this cake, and it was part of Christmas watching her do it. All the performance of lining the tin with paper, masses of it all around the sides and on top – and then sitting up all night waiting for it to come out. I swear she sat up because it was the only time, just before the Christmas rush, when she had five minutes to herself. The cake was always moist and heavy with fruit and when I took over 'doing Christmas' I took over the recipe. I have added bits and we are still happy with the end product which does not need months to mature. I make it about the beginning or middle of November.

8 oz (225 g) butter

8 oz (225 g) soft brown sugar

up to 2½ lb (1.1 kg) fruit; I use
   12 oz (350 g) currants,
   8 oz (225 g) sultanas,
   4 oz (110 g) muscadets,
   12 oz (350 g) raisins

8 oz (225 g) flour, with a good pinch
   of salt

6 oz (175 g) cherries

4 large eggs, beaten

½–1 tsp mixed spice

1 tbsp black treacle (warm the spoon first)

4 oz (110 g) ground almonds

2 oz (50 g) walnuts or almonds

4 oz (110 g) mixed peel

juice of 1 large lemon

grated nutmeg

Grease and line an 8 in (20 cm) square or round tin (preferably loose-bottomed) with double-thick greaseproof paper to stand 4 in (10 cm) above the rim. Cream the butter until soft and add the sugar; cream until pale. Dust the fruit with flour and cut the cherries in half. Add the beaten eggs and sifted flour to the butter mixture. Then add treacle, fruit, cherries, ground almonds, nuts, spices and lemon juice. Mix well and pile into the tin. Cover the top with double greaseproof paper resting it on the edging paper. My mother cooked her cake for 7 hours at 250 F (120 C) Reg ½. I cook mine for 6–8 hours in the cool oven of my Aga at 250–275 F (125–140 C) Reg ½–1. When a skewer comes out clean it is cooked. It is really a matter of checking until it's done. I make holes all over mine when it is just cooked, then pour over good Spanish brandy and leave it in the tin to cool. Turn out and wrap in several layers of greaseproof paper and then foil and keep until it is time to marzipan.

SHORTBREAD

(MAKES 8–10 PIECES)

This is my favourite shortbread recipe. I prefer it made with icing sugar rather than caster and this recipe is very rich.

8 oz (225 g) flour
4 oz (110 g) icing sugar
4 oz (110 g) cornflour
8 oz (225 g) butter, softened

Sift the flour, icing sugar and cornflour into a large basin and add the butter. Mix with fingertips only, rubbing until the mixture resembles fine crumbs. Continue until the dough starts sticking in large lumps. Turn onto a cold, lightly floured board and knead lightly. Press this mixture into a 9 in (23 cm) round sandwich cake tin, press the edges down to 'flute' them and prick all over with a fork. Bake in a moderate oven at 350 F (180 C) Reg 4 for about 1 hour. It should be a lovely pale golden brown when cooked. Remove from oven and score with a knife into sections – let it cool in the tin.

GRANNIE T's FLIP

(MAKES 12–14 PIECES)

Grannie T, our lovely nanny from Yorkshire, is not allowed out of our house unless she leaves tinfuls of this recipe. I have never found a child who did not beg for a second piece and it is very good for Bonfire Night.

2 oz (50 g) butter
2 oz (50 g) margarine
4 oz (110 g) granulated sugar
1 tbsp syrup
2 oz (50 g) self-raising flour
2½ oz (65 g) cornflakes
½ oz (15 g) coconut
2 oz (50 g) Quaker Oats

Melt the butter and margarine, sugar and syrup. Do not overheat. Mix all the dry ingredients in a bowl and pour over syrup mixture, mixing well. Bake in a greased swiss roll tin in a moderate oven until pale brown and crispy-looking. Remove from heat and cut into segments in tin. Leave to cool a little and then cool in pieces on cooling tray.

CHOCOLATE BISCUIT FINGERS

(MAKES 15–20)

I came across a lovely chocolate cookbook some three years ago *(Cadbury's Chocolate Cookbook)* and have tried many of their recipes since. I lived as a child in Birmingham, indeed went to school with several of the Cadbury girls and part of our education was a trip to the factory. Contrary to the well-known saying 'the more you eat, the less you like', we all stuffed ourselves with chocolate and I've loved it ever since. Forget all but a few of the foreign makes, it takes a lot to beat Cadburys milk and Rowntrees or Terrys dark chocolate.

The Cadburys business began when a young Quaker, John Cadbury, opened a shop in Birmingham in 1824 mainly to sell tea and coffee but also to introduce the cocoa bean and hot chocolate to an unsuspecting Birmingham public. It was a huge success. This finger biscuit fudge is lovely and has the added bonus of being able to use up any broken biscuits that are left in the tin.

4 oz (110 g) butter
2 tbsp golden syrup
8 oz (225 g) sweet biscuits
1 oz (25 g) raisins
2 oz (50 g) glacé cherries, quartered
5 oz (150 g) Bournville plain chocolate, chopped into pieces
5 oz (150 g) Bournville plain chocolate, for melting
knob butter

Melt the butter and syrup in a saucepan over a low heat. Rough crush the biscuits and then the raisins, cherries and chopped chocolate. Stir well together and press firmly into a swiss roll tin which has been greased and lined. Leave overnight to harden. Turn out to ice. Melt the Bournville chocolate over a bowl of hot water, add 1 tbsp water and a small knob of butter and melt until smooth. Spread this over the top of the biscuit and fork up in swirls. Leave to harden and then cut into fingers.

CHERRY CAKE

Full of cherries, moist and delicious, this was made for us by a previous housekeeper and I liked it enough to beg the recipe. The amounts are either for an 8 in (20 cm) or 5 in (13 cm) tin.

8 in (20 cm)
18 oz (500 g) glace cherries
8 oz (225 g) butter
8 oz (225g) caster sugar
3 eggs
½ tsp vanilla essence
1 tsp baking powder
4 oz (110 g) ground almonds
10 oz (275 g) flour
1 oz (25 g) flaked almonds
¼ tsp salt
5 in (13 cm)
8 oz (225 g) glacé cherries
3 oz (75 g) butter
3 oz (75 g) caster sugar
1 egg plus 1 yolk
few drops vanilla essence
½ tsp baking powder
2 oz (50 g) ground almonds
5 oz (150 g) flour
½ tsp (15 g) flaked almonds
good pinch salt

Rinse the cherries in boiling water and drain. Keep out 10 (5) for top. Halve the rest. Beat the butter and sugar until pale and creamy, add beaten eggs and vanilla essence. Stir in cherries and ground almonds. Sift the flour, baking powder and salt and stir into the mixture. Spoon this into a prepared (greased and lined) tin and sprinkle the almonds in strips on the top. Bake the 8 in (20 cm) cake at

350 F (180 C) for 1 hour. Quarter remaining cherries and arrange on the cake top between the almond strips. Lower heat to 325 F (160 C) Reg 3 for a further 1½ hours and cover the cake with greaseproof paper for the last 45 minutes. Cool in the tin. Bake the 5 in (13 cm) cake in the same manner as the 8 in (20 cm) for the first hour then reduce heat, add cherries and cool for further 30–40 minutes.

JOC's LEMON CAKE

This is from Yorkshire days – Jocelyn Frazier was famed for her lemon cake and there was always a rush at coffee mornings to buy her cakes. She gave me the recipe before I left – it's moist, lemony and delicious.

6 oz (175 g) butter
6 oz (175 g) caster sugar
3 large eggs, beaten
6 oz (175 g) self-raising flour, sifted
Syrup
4 oz (110 g) granulated sugar
juice of 3 lemons plus grated rind

Cream butter and sugar until soft and pale lemon coloured – add beaten eggs and sifted flour and mix gently. Add 1 tbsp boiling water and mix well for 1 minute. Turn mixture into a well greased 7 in (18 cm) or 8 in (20 cm) cake tin. I put a circle of greaseproof paper in mine, it makes getting it out much easier. Bake at 325 F (160 C) Reg 3 for about 1 hour, until cake is cooked and springy to touch. Make syrup by boiling granulated sugar, lemon juice and grated rind, then simmer for 10 minutes. Turn cake out upside down onto a hot plate and pour the hot syrup all over the top. It freezes beautifully.

PARKIN

We moved into our farmhouse in Yorkshire on Bonfire Night 1970 – an auspicious night, dry and clear and the sky ablaze with stars. Colin Geddes, the head greenkeeper, had built a huge bonfire just beyond our garden gate for all his greenkeeping staff and we joined the party to be fortified by well-laced punch, hot potatoes and parkin.

This parkin has travelled with me. It much improves with keeping and the combination of oatmeal and flour and thick brown treacle is essentially Northern. I must confess, I normally use syrup, which I find just as good.

6 oz (175 g) flour
1½ tsp bicarbonate of soda
1 tsp ground ginger
2 oz (50 g) medium oatmeal
3 oz (75 g) brown sugar
3 oz (75 g) butter or margarine
4 oz (110 g) syrup or brown treacle
1 egg, beaten
little milk

Sift the flour, bicarbonate of soda and ginger into a basin. Mix in the oatmeal. Melt sugar, butter and syrup and when melted pour over dry ingredients in bowl. Add the egg and just enough milk to get a soft dropping consistency. Spoon into a well greased and lined deep flan tin

—or, in Yorkshire, a Yorkshire pudding tin – and cook for about 1 hour at 325 F (160 C) Reg 3 until firm to touch. Cool in the tin and then remove and cut into squares. Put into an airtight container and keep for two weeks. If you like the taste of orange try adding candied orange peel and grated orange rind to the basic mixture.

YORKSHIRE CURD TART

(SERVES 6)

This is another Yorkshire recipe. It took me a long time and a lot of trying to find a recipe that seemed closest to the mouthwatering delicate tarts we used to buy at our favourite baker in Moortown, Leeds. This is the closest yet.

6 oz (175 g) sweet shortcrust pastry

1 oz (25 g) butter, melted

2 oz (50 g) caster sugar

2 eggs, separated

grated rind of 1 lemon

1 oz (25 g) currants

8 oz (225 g) curd cheese

pinch nutmeg, freshly ground

Carefully roll out the pastry and line an 8 in (20 cm) round flat ring. Mix the butter, caster sugar, egg yolks, lemon rind, fruit and cheese together. Whisk the egg whites until stiff and fold into the mixture. Fill the pastry case and sprinkle with nutmeg. Cook for about 30 minutes at 375 F (190 C) Reg 5. Check to see that filling is set. If the pastry is browning too quickly, reduce the heat to 350 F (180 C) Reg 4. Serve hot or cold. This recipe

works well for individual tartlets too, but obviously they cook more quickly, so keep a close eye on them.

COFFEE AND WALNUT CAKE

This is my personal favourite. I like chocolate cake but the combination of coffee and walnuts is, to me, far more tempting and this cake is moist, very rich and deliciously fattening.

6 oz (175 g) butter

6 oz (175 g) pale soft brown sugar

3 eggs

6 oz (175 g) self-raising flour

3 oz (75 g) walnuts, chopped into small pieces

2 tbsp Camp coffee essence

Filling and icing

4 oz (110 g) butter

6 oz (175 g) icing sugar, sifted

3 tbsp very strong coffee or Camp essence

12 walnut halves

Grease and line an 8 in (20 cm) cake tin. Cream the butter and sugar until light and fluffy, and gradually beat in the eggs. Sift in the flour and fold in, then fold in walnuts and coffee essence. Bake at 350 F (180 C) Reg 4 for 25 minutes or until cooked. Cake should leave the sides of the tin and spring back when pressed lightly in the middle. Turn out and cool. To make the filling, cream the butter and icing sugar gradually adding the coffee. Cream until smooth. Split the cake in half and sandwich together with half the filling. Then spread the top with the remainder. Decorate with a circle of walnut halves and grated chocolate.

BARA BRITH

A teatime cake to slice and butter.
There are many different versions of
this recipe, which means speckled
bread and is Celtic in its origins. My
recipe came from Robbie Thomas, a
great friend and wife of David
Thomas, also a professional golfer of
the same era as my husband. When I
was a young bride, she already had
three hungry young boys and David
to feed and one of my clearest
memories was lunch before a
Manchester United match at Old
Trafford. A dustbin-sized dish of
cottage pie was wheeled in – I'd never
seen so much food consumed. She
made masses of Bara Brith, four at a
time, and baked tins of fudge,
biscuits, and other such 'fillers'. As
all three of her boys grew to well over
six foot tall, there must be a moral
somewhere!

1½ lb (675 g) mixed fruit
8 oz (225 g) demerara sugar
¾ pt (425 ml) strong cold tea
1 lb (450 g) self-raising flour
1 large egg

Prepare two loaf tins, grease and line
the bottom with silicone paper. Soak
the mixed fruit, sugar and tea and
leave overnight or for a morning.
Then stir in the self-raising flour and
egg. Divide mixture between the tins
and cook for about 1–1¼ hrs in a
moderate oven. Test with a skewer.
slice and butter to serve. It freezes
beautifully.

LOS ANGELES CARROT CAKE

Recipes for carrot cake are numerous
– all different and each owner swears
theirs is the best! I've tried many, but
always come back to this one; the
banana helps to keep the cake moist.

8 oz (225 g) self-raising flour
2 tsp baking powder
4 oz (110 g) pale soft brown sugar
2 oz (50 g) walnuts, chopped
4 oz (110 g) carrots, English winter ones – full of flavour
2 ripe bananas
2 eggs, beaten
¼ pt (150 ml) corn oil
Icing
3 oz (75 g) butter
3 oz (75 g) cream cheese
6 oz (175 g) icing sugar, sifted
vanilla essence
half walnuts to decorate

Grease and line an 8 in (20 cm) cake
tin. Sift the flour and baking powder
into a large bowl. Add the sugar and
chopped walnuts and stir. Peel and
grate the carrots and add to mixture.
Skin and mash the bananas and add
with the beaten eggs and oil. Blend
well to get a soft dropping
consistency. Put into prepared tin
and cook for approximately 1 hour at
350 F (180 C) Reg 4. Cake should be
golden, firm and nicely risen. Turn
out and cool. To make the icing,
soften the butter, add the cream

cheese, icing sugar and a few drops of
vanilla essence. Beat until smooth
and creamy. When the cake is cold,
spread icing over the top and down
sides, rough up with a fork and
decorate with walnuts.

P. J.'s HARVEST FLAN

Our housekeeper, Norma, fondly
known to one and all as P. J. (don't
ask me why!), makes quantities of
deliciously filling biscuits, buns and
cakes. This recipe is one of hers. It's
much better with home-made
shortcrust pastry. I fact I have given
up making traditional apple pies as
hers are so much nicer.

8 oz (225 g) shortcrust pastry

Filling

4 oz (110 g) butter

4 oz (110 g) caster sugar

2 large eggs, beaten

8 oz (225 g) dessicated coconut

good raspberry jam

Line a 12 in (30 cm) or 2 x 6 in
(15 cm) or 7 in (180 cm) flan dish(es)
with the pastry (preferably a loose
bottomed tin). Cover the bottom with
the jam. Cream the butter and sugar
until light and fluffy and gradually
add 1 beaten egg followed by 1 tbsp
coconut to prevent curdling. Add the
second egg and then stir in remaining
coconut. Put the mixture into a flan
tin making sure the jam is covered.
Make lattice-work strips with any
remaining pastry. Cook in a fairly hot
oven for 30 minutes or until mixture
is golden brown. This flan is delicious
served cold in fingers with ice cream
on top.

P. J.'s MAID OF HONOUR TARTS
(MAKES 6–8)

I love these, they remind me of our
Yorkshire days and they are said to
have been a favourite of Anne Boleyn
from her time at Hampton Court
Palace as a Maid of Honour to
Catherine of Aragon. The curds have
to drain, so begin preparations the
day before you need them.

8 oz (225 g) puff pastry

Filling

1 pt (575 ml) fresh milk

1 tsp rennet

pinch salt

4 oz (110 g) butter

2 egg yolks

2 tsp brandy

½ oz (15 g) sweet almonds, blanched

little sugar

little fresh nutmeg

rind and juice of ½ lemon

currants to decorate

Warm the milk to blood heat, add the
rennet and a pinch of salt. When the
curds have set, put them into a fine
muslin cloth, draw up the corners
and hang overnight for the liquid to
drain out. Roll out the pastry and line
6–8 lightly greased patty tins with it.
Rub the curds through a sieve with
the butter into a bowl. Beat the egg
yolks with the brandy until frothy
and then add to the curds. Chop the
almonds and then add the sugar,
nutmeg, lemon rind and juice. Fill the
pastry-lined patty tins with the
mixture and sprinkle generously with
currants. Bake at 425 F (220 C) Reg
7 for about 20–25 minutes. They

should be puffed up and golden brown and are delicious eaten piping hot straight from the oven!

GOOEY CHOCOLATE CAKE

Rich and totally irresistible and always a success, chocolate cake must be the one thing everyone loves. Chocolate came to Europe in 1519 and the French and English became early addicts. Chocolate should be melted very slowly over a pan of hot water, if it gets too hot it stiffens and becomes unworkable. Have you ever tried Mars Bars melted this way? They make the most heavenly sauce for ice cream!

8 oz (225 g) butter, softened
8 oz (225 g) caster sugar
3 large eggs, beaten
6 oz (175 g) self-raising flour
2 oz (50 g) cocoa powder
½ tsp baking powder
2 tbsp milk
Filling
¼ pt (150 ml) double cream
6 oz (175 g) plain Bournville chocolate, grated

Grease and line the bases of 2 x 7 in (18 cm) 8 in (20 cm) deep sandwich tins. Cream the butter and sugar until light and fluffy. Gradually beat in the eggs, mixing well between each addition. Sift the flour, cocoa and baking powder and then fold carefully into the mixture with the milk. Divide into the two tins and cook for 25–30 minutes at 350 F (180 C) Reg 4 until firm to touch.

Cool slightly and turn out onto a wire rack to cool. They are better wrapped and left overnight before filling. To make the filling, put the cream in a pan, scald and remove from the heat. Stir in the chocolate (grated to make it melt more easily) until it is melted and smooth. Leave to cool and thicken, stirring often. When thick enough to spread, carefully slice each cake horizontally in half and use half the cream to sandwich the layers together, use the remainder to spread over the top and sides. Leave to set ina cool place. I cover the top with chocolate drops for the children, or, for an adult tea, make some chocolate curls. Using a vegetable peeler (the sort with a flexible blade) I peel along the flat side of a block of good dark chocolate. But be careful as they are very fragile.

ROD's FARMHOUSE LOAF CAKE

This is my hairdresser's wife's cake. He has a long day with no time to eat – what demanding people we ladies are! So Joan sends him to work with thick chunks of this cake. She did say that the mix of butter and Blueband is very important.

7 oz (200 g) self-raising flour
½ tsp mixed spice
pinch salt
6 oz (175 g) butter and Blueband mixed
6 oz (175 g) light brown sugar
2 large eggs plus 1 yolk
1 tbsp mollasses or black treacle
1 tbsp brandy
1 tbsp milk

3–4 oz (75–110 g) fruit, washed
and dried

2 oz (50 g) cherries

walnut halves and cherries for top

Sieve together the flour, mixed spice and salt and set aside. Cream fat and sugar until fluffy. Add eggs, then molasses, beating lightly. Fold in the sieved dry ingredients, then add the brandy and milk. Add fruit and cherries. Put the mixture in a greased and lined loaf tin and the walnuts and a few cherries on top. Bake in a pre-heated oven at 260 F (130 C) Reg ¾ for 1½ hours (it may need an extra few minutes).

APRICOT TEA BREAD

This is a recipe I picked up in a magazine. I've had it for years and it works just as well with tinned apricots, well drained, in fact the tinned variety keep the cake just that bit more moist.

6 oz (175 g) self-raising flour

pinch salt

½ tsp ground nutmeg

3 oz (75 g) butter

3 oz (75 g) soft brown sugar

4 oz (110 g) dried apricots, finely
chopped

2 tbsp treacle

3–5 tbsp milk

1 large egg, lightly beaten

Grease and prepare a loaf tin of about 1½ pt (800 ml) capacity. Sift together the flour, salt and nutmeg and rub in the butter. Add sugar and apricots. Blend together the treacle, milk and egg and mix with the dry ingredients and put into a greased and lined rectangular loaf tin. Bake in the centre of the oven at 350 F (180 C) Reg 4 for about 1 hour. Allow to cool. Serve sliced and buttered. It freezes beautifully.

QUICK LUNCH AND SUPPER DISHES

Here are some simple recipes, all of which can be made quickly. We are great ones for cauliflower cheeses, which I make by separating the florets and lightly cooking in salted water, drain and cover with a good thick creamy sauce with lots of strong cheese and a good teaspoon of mustard. Then I top it with bacon rolls, mushrooms with a knob of butter inside them and halved tomatoes, covering the whole thing with grated Gruyère and biscuit crumbs. Into the Aga for 20 minutes and it is hot, delicious and filling.

SWISS ONION TART

(SERVES 6)

This is from my Swiss days, Madame Cuénoud and long lunches with fellow students all talking at once. We used to eat it with Dandelion Salad, so I've given you the recipe for this as well.

1 lb (450 g) large French onions, peeled and finely sliced
2 oz (50 g) butter
1 dsp soft brown sugar
juice of 1 lemon
8 oz (225 g) rich shortcrust pastry
8 oz (225 g) double cream
2 eggs
seasoning
extra butter

Take the onions and sweat over low heat in the butter, soft brown sugar and lemon juice. Meanwhile line an 8 in (20 cm) flan ring with rich shortcrust pastry. When onions are soft and transparent, drain and combine them with the cream, well beaten with the eggs and seasoning to taste. Pour into prepared pastry case and dot with the butter. Bake at 500 F (250 C) Reg 10 for 5 minutes then lower to 375 F (190 C) Reg 5 for 20–25 minutes until set and golden brown.

DANDELION SALAD

(SERVES 4–6)

You need the young spring dandelions, picked fresh when the leaves are tender.

2 oz (250 g) green bacon, diced.
½ oz (60 g) butter
3 eggs, hardboiled and chopped up
8 oz (250 g) dandelion leaves
about 4 fl oz (110 ml) French dressing
small clove garlic

Fry the bacon in the butter over low heat until golden brown and crispy. Rub the salad bowl over with the bruised garlic clove and pour in French dressing, add eggs. Add dandelions and hot bacon, toss and eat immediately.

CHICORY AND HAM ROLLS

(SERVES 6)

By chicory I mean the bulby long-leaved vegetable which some call endive. It's not to everyone's liking so you can substitute with leeks.

12 small chicory
12 slices thinly sliced cooked ham
1 pt (575 ml) well-flavoured Béchamel sauce with the following added: ¼ pt (150 ml) cream salt, freshly ground black pepper freshly ground nutmeg
1½ oz (40 g) Gruyère or Cheddar cheese, grated

Butter a shallow ovenproof dish, large enough to hold the endive rolls. Put the chicory into a saucepan, cover with boiling salted water and cook until just soft. Drain well and cool. Wrap each chicory in a slice of ham and arrange these rolls in the prepared dish. Pour over the prepared sauce and sprinkle the top with cheese (I also use biscuit crumbs), dot with butter and bake at 275 F (140 C) Reg 1 for about 30 minutes, until the sauce is bubbling and the top crisp. Serve immediately with crusty bread.

KEDGEREE BLENHEIM PALACE

(SERVES 3–4)

My Father's temper could be short. How well I remember the Christmas when, with a full complement of relatives on Boxing Night, Mother served kedgeree and Father lost his temper. We all were sitting round the huge log fire in the drawing room recovering from the past 24 hours of fun and festivities. 'A light supper on our knees,' my Mother declared! Mother dispensed the food, Father the white wine. Mother in her wisdom put Father's plate on his chair and, horror of horrors, he sat on it. There was total shocked silence for half a minute and then one of us children laughed. That was it, Father exploded, the food went into the bin and Father retired to his study and was not seen again that night. Every time I eat kedgeree now, I'm tempted to chuckle.

This recipe I found in a magazine years ago. It was made, so the story went, for the 10th Duke of Marlborough who loved its creamy taste for breakfast.

6 oz (175 g) long-grain rice (preferably Patna)
6 oz (175 g) cooked Finnan Haddock, de-skinned, boned and flaked
2 hard-boiled eggs, chopped
parsley to decorate
Sauce
1 oz (25 g) butter
1 oz (25 g) flour
1 pt (575 ml) stock (cube)
3 eggs
4 tbsp double cream

Have ready a pan of boiling salted water and tip in the long-grain rice. Boil rapidly for 15 minutes and, when cooked, drain. Mix the rice with the Finnan Haddock. Add the hard-boiled eggs and stir in the sauce. To make this, melt the butter in a pan. Add the flour and gradually add the stock. Bring gently to the boil stirring all the time to prevent lumps and to ensure the floury taste has gone. (Most people never cook sauces long enough to cook the flour). Tip the sauce into either a double saucepan or into a bowl resting over a pan of water. Add the eggs beaten up with the double cream. Heat the sauce whipping all the time but do not let it boil, otherwise it will curdle. When nicely thickened, mix into the rice and fish and put into a pretty shallow dish and warm in the oven. Lots of parsley over the top, lots of hot toast and it's quite superb.

FILLET OF PORK NORMANDY

(SERVES 6)

A marvellously versatile piece of meat is a fillet of pork. One can roast it, braise it, stuff it with apples and raisins, or grapes and nuts or good old sage and onion stuffing. It's also delicious cooked as a quick supper dish with smooth creamy potatoes and a green salad.

2 lb (900 g) fillet of pork
seasoned flour
½ pt (275 ml) dry white wine
½ pt (275 ml) button mushrooms, sliced
1½ oz (40 g) butter
2 tbsp brandy
¼ pt (150 ml) double cream
lots of chopped parsley
seasoning

Cut the pork into medallions. First remove any surplus fat or sinew. Toss in seasoned flour and set aside. Put the wine into a small pan and bring to the boil, add mushrooms and simmer covered for about 12 minutes. Melt butter in small frying pan and brown the meat. Meanwhile heat the brandy and, when warm, set alight; when the flames die down tip it into the meat and stir well to get the nice bits off the bottom of the pan. Add wine and mushrooms, cover with a close-fitting lid and simmer gently in the oven for about 35 minutes. The meat must be tender. Place the meat and mushrooms into a shallow serving dish and add the cream and some parsley to the juices remaining in the pan. Simmer until the sauce starts to thicken and check the seasoning. Tip the sauce over the meat and serve with lots of parsley.

LEEKS WITH GRUYÈRE AND BACON

(SERVES 4)

This recipe is from my Swiss days and uses my favourite cheese, Gruyère. Anything with this cheese pleases me, and at home we all love leeks.

1½ lb (675 g) medium-sized firm leeks
6 oz (175 g) lean bacon
½ oz (15 g) butter
seasoning
6 oz (175 g) Gruyère cheese, grated
½ pt (275 ml) chicken stock

Trim the leeks and slash them crossways down to the white part and wash very thoroughly to remove all the dirt and grit. Cut into 2–3 in (5–7 cm) lengths and blanch in boiling salted water until nearly cooked but still crisp. Drain well making sure all the water is out of them. Cool. De-rind and chop the bacon in pieces. Choose a shallow ovenproof gratin dish and butter generously. Put a layer of leeks on the bottom, season and sprinkle with bacon and grated cheese. Continue these layers finishing with a layer of cheese. Pour the stock down the sides and bake at 375 F (190 C) Reg 5 for about 30 minutes. The leeks should be tender and the topping crusted and brown. Serve immediately with crusty toast or French bread.

QUICK CHEESE SOUFFLÉ

(SERVES 4)

This I often make. Believe it or not, the recipe came from an old free leaflet and is totally foolproof!

3 large egg yolks
4 oz (110 g) Cheddar cheese, grated
3 egg whites, stiffly beaten
Sauce
2 oz (50 g) butter
½ pt (275 ml) milk
2 oz (50 g) flour
½ tsp salt
¼ tsp cayenne pepper
¼ tsp dry mustard

Prepare a 2 pt (1.1 l) soufflé dish with melted butter. To make the sauce, sieve together the flour, salt, pepper and mustard. Melt butter and add dry ingredients, blend slowly. Add in milk until you have a smooth consistency and then take off the heat. Whisk the egg yolks into the sauce, fold in the grated cheese and lastly, using a metal spoon, fold in the beaten egg whites. Pour into soufflé dish and cook on a baking tray on the middle shelf at 375 F (190 C) Reg 5 for about 40–45 minutes. When ready it should be well risen and golden brown on the top, soft and light in the centre. Serve immediately with hot toast.

EGGS FLORENTINE

(SERVES 4)

This is one of Peter's favourites; it reminds me of arriving in Hong Kong, hot, tired and dusty after hours of travelling from Los Angeles. Our hotel was peaceful with a spectacular view over Hong Kong Harbour and in those days the ferries still bustled backwards and forward. We ordered Egg and Prawn Florentine and I am convinced that it was the best we've ever eaten. To the basic recipe below try, for a change, putting a layer of peeled and cooked king prawns on top of the eggs before putting the sauce over the top.

1½ lb (700 g) fresh spinach
salt, pepper and nutmeg, freshly ground
1 oz (25 g) butter
4 soft-boiled fresh eggs
1 tbsp grated cheese, preferably Gruyère
Sauce
½ oz (15 g) butter
½ oz (15 g) flour
¼ pt (150 ml) milk
¼ pt (150 ml) single cream
salt and pepper
nutmeg

Wash the spinach well, de-stalk and cook in boiling water. Drain thoroughly and chop. Add seasoning and nutmeg and butter. Butter a fireproof dish and put in the spinach. Place the soft-boiled eggs on top. Make the sauce by melting the butter, blending in the flour and slowly adding the milk and single cream. Cook till thick and creamy smooth. Season with salt, pepper and nutmeg. Cover the spinach and eggs generously with it. Sprinkle with the grated cheese and pop into hot oven for 10 minutes to heat and crisp the top.

SALLY's FLAMICHE

(SERVES 4)

My sister uses this leek dish often and I begged the recipe off her. She says it's ideal for a busy working mum.

3 oz (75 g) butter
1½ lb (700 g) leeks, well washed and sliced
8 thin sausages
3 eggs
¼ pt (150 ml) double cream
salt and black pepper
12 oz (350 g) puff pastry (I use a packet)
1 beaten egg yolk

Melt the butter in a pan and gently sweat the leeks, covering for about 30 minutes until they are very soft and puréed. Take lid off and put on a higher heat to evaporate the liquid, remove and leave to cool. Meanwhile cook the sausages until golden brown. Drain on kitchen paper. Beat the eggs, cream and seasoning and mix in leek mixture. Divide pastry in

half, roll each into a 10 in (25 cm) circle. Put one on to a baking sheet. Pile on mixture, leaving a 1 in (2.5 cm) border and arrange the sausages in a star on top. Dampen the border, place the second circle of pastry on top and press down at the edges to seal. Cut slits in the top and brush with beaten egg. Cook for 10 minutes at 425 F (220 C) Reg 7 and then lower to 350 F (180 C) Reg 4 for a further 30 minutes. If it cooks too quickly, cover the top with foil.

CHILLED LEMON FLAN

(SERVES 6–8)

This came from Caroline Gammon, wife of Peter Gammon, owner of Trevose Golf and Country Club, near Padstow in North Cornwall. Their lovely home is one of my husband's favourite boltholes. In the relaxed atmosphere he can play golf at his leisure with old chums and their hospitality is warm and much treasured by us both. The children love the long wide beaches, sand dunes and fresh air; sadly we don't get there often enough. This recipe is double quantity to use a 14 oz (400 g) tin of condensed milk. Use one and freeze the second without its final layer of cream.

8 oz (225 g) digestive biscuits, crushed
4 oz (110 g) butter, melted
1 tbsp caster sugar
Filling
½ pt (275 ml) double cream
14 oz (400 g) tin condensed milk
rind of 4 lemons, finely grated, and juice
6 oz (175 g) double cream for topping

Mix together the biscuits, melted butter and caster sugar and press into two 7 in (18 cm) tins or flan dishes. Bake for 8 minutes and cool. To make the filling, mix the double cream into the condensed milk. Add the lemon rind, plus the juice, slowly beaten in. Pour into the bases and leave to set. When ready to serve, lightly whip double cream and pour over the top. Grate chocolate over the cream, which pleases the children – there is rarely any left.

BANANA UPSIDE-DOWN PUDDING

(SERVES 6–8)

This is a cold-evening pud. When the children come home from school, I nearly always have a 'soup' going in the bottom of the Aga, full of vegetables, pearl barley, any meat bone I can get from the butcher. A bowl of soup, followed by this pud and lots of custard, is perfect.

2 bananas
4 oz (110 g) butter or good margarine
4 oz (110 g) caster sugar
2 large eggs
4 oz (110 g) self-raising flour
1 tsp baking powder
Caramel
6 oz (175 g) granulated sugar
10 tbsp water

Make the caramel by mixing the sugar and water. Stir without boiling until sugar dissolves, then without stirring boil hard until mixture turns golden brown. Pour this into an 8 in (20 cm) sandwich tin. When caramel is starting to set, arrange bananas either in 'pennies' or cut lengthwise like the spokes of a wheel. Make the pudding by mixing butter and sugar until soft and creamy, add the eggs with a spoonful of flour, mix, then add the rest of the baking powder and flour sieved together and beat until smooth; add a tiny amount of milk if the mixture is too firm. Spread on to the caramel and banana and bake at 350 F (180 C) Reg 4 for 35–40 minutes. Remove and turn out onto a plate.

INDEX TO RECIPES

ACKNOWLEDGEMENTS

My thanks to the following sources for recipes which have become personal favourites:

Elizabeth Ayrton, *English Provincial Cookery*; *Cadbury's Chocolate Cookbook*; Denis Curtis, *Sunday Telegraph*; Paul Jeanroy, *Bon Appétit*.

Thanks also to those who contributed photographs of their particular specialities:

Dormy Hotel, Ferndown; Golf View Hotel, Nairn; Old Thorns Golf and Country Club, Liphook; Pool Court Restaurant, Otley; Turnberry Hotel.

And finally, a special thank you to:

Richard Cobham, who photographed my own creations; to Heather McInerney, who helped me prepare them for the camera; and to Peter Hale, who drew the cartoon on page 78.